"**D**ONALD MCLEAN, of Polk County, Florida, told a Senate committee that since phosphate plants began putting seven tons of fluorides a day into the air he has had to sell his cattle and his citrus groves because the cattle sickened and died, crops that used to mature in 80 days now take 200, barbed wire that used to last 20 years rots in 4, and he doesn't dare grow vegetables for his family for fear they will pick up the same chemicals that fall onto his pastures and groves. 'It eats up the paint and etches glass, it kills trees, it kills cattle. It is an irritant to mucous membrane, and we have sore throats, tears run out of our eyes, we sneeze, we have nosebleeds. Gentlemen, am I a fool to assume that that stuff [is] injurious to humans?' "

—from "No Place to Hide"
by Ben H. Bagdikian

Air and water pollution are insidiously maiming every person in the United States as well as our most precious resources.

Robert T. Moorefield

With selections by:

Rachel Carson
Robert F. Kennedy
John Bird
Luther L. Terry, M.D.

PROBLEMS OF AMERICAN SOCIETY

Focusing on the urban scene, youth, the individual and his search for a better life, the books in this series probe the most crucial dilemmas of our time.

*Forthcoming

GERALD
LEINWAND
assisted by
Gerald Popkin

Air
and Water
Pollution

WSP
WASHINGTON SQUARE PRESS · NEW YORK

AIR AND WATER POLLUTION

A *Washington Square Press* edition
1st printing .... September, 1969

WSP

Published by
Washington Square Press, Inc., 630 Fifth Avenue, New York, N.Y.

WASHINGTON SQUARE PRESS editions are distributed in the U.S. by Simon & Schuster, Inc., 630 Fifth Avenue, New York, N.Y. 10020 and in Canada by Simon & Schuster of Canada, Ltd., Richmond Hill, Ontario, Canada.

L

1 2 3 4 5 1 0 9.

*To my parents
who taught me to live
in urban America*

ACKNOWLEDGMENT

This is one of a series of volumes designed to become text materials for urban schools. Partially funded under Title I, Elementary and Secondary Education Act, Public Law 89–10, 1965, the series grew out of a curriculum development project conceived and executed by the editor. Washington Square Press and the Curriculum Committee of the Trenton, New Jersey, public schools provided valuable editorial assistance.

Mrs. Bernice Munce is Project Supervisor of the Curriculum Committee which includes the following members: William Carter, Elsie Collins, Albert De-Martin, Harold P. DuShane, Barbara Hancock, Roland Hence, Steven McLaine, Gerald Popkin, Richard Scheetz, Carol West.

Also contributing to the effort were Neil O'Donnel, Joseph Fonseca and Eugene Winchester as research assistants, Mrs. Eileen Donohue as secretary, and my wife who spent hours typing and proofreading.

Preface

One of the dilemmas of our time is that man who knows how to reach outer space and will eventually send men to the moon does not know how to keep the air he breathes or the water he drinks pure enough to sustain life and assure good health. Most problems of urban society are difficult to solve largely because they have their origins outside the city itself. Problems of crime, poverty, slums, drug addiction, riots or mental illness are as much social problems as they are urban problems. They cannot be solved by focusing on the city alone.

The problems of air and water pollution appear to be different. For one thing, to a greater extent than other urban problems they are indeed related to the geographically fixed industrial centers of any urban region. For another, in most problems of urban society, while we have the will to solve them, we lack the know-how. In the case of air and water pollution, we seem to have the know-how, yet appear to lack the will. We do have at our fingertips the technological ability to provide clean air and fresh water. We do know, or can readily find out, who the chief polluters are, and what we must do to penalize them or to insist that appropriate steps be taken to eliminate the sources of pollution.

Preface

Like the other volumes in this series on *Problems of American Society,* this is an introductory study. We have tried to present the problem simply and nontechnically. Our aim has been to make some contribution, however small, to create the will and the climate in which problems of air and water pollution can be solved. It is hoped that this book will help its readers develop a clearer insight into the nature of the problem and perhaps encourage them to do something about it.

The readings in this volume were chosen to illustrate various approaches to the problems of air and water pollution and to raise questions as to why they exist and why they have resisted efforts to solve them. The readings try to show that some men have long been concerned with eliminating air and water pollution, but that the general public has remained essentially apathetic. The questions which follow each reading are designed to help readers identify the problem for themselves and to encourage them to think about the kind of action that can be taken and the kind of action that *they* can take. While this book parallels the others in this series it differs in one respect. More than the others, it is action oriented. That is, in the introductory essay, in the readings, and in the questions, the primary focus is to encourage not only thinking but doing as well. Only the future will tell us whether this hoped-for result has been achieved.

G. L.

Contents

Contents

Part One

The Problem and the Challenge

New York City, Thanksgiving, 1966—An inverted air mass causing heavy stagnant air pollution chokes the metropolitan area. Here the air pollution index is 43.4 (an index of 50 is the danger level). (Charles Steinacker, Black Star)

ON the morning of November 24, 1966, New Yorkers awoke to observe Thanksgiving. The usual parades and family dinners that mark the day had all been planned. But something unusual happened, something that the people of New York City had not planned. An inverted air mass had settled over the city. An inverted air mass is an unusual weather condition that does not allow the smoke and soot from the city to rise. These poisonous gases are not released until a wind allows the stale, smoke-filled air to be carried away.

How serious is this? Dirty, polluted air can be very serious. New Yorkers had been warned that if the mass of foul air did not move, a "smog alert" would have to be declared. If this happened people with heart and breathing ailments would be advised to remain indoors. Private cars would not be allowed on the streets so that the exhausts from their engines would not be added to already dirty air. Office and apartment buildings would also be forced to shut down their incinerators and to lower their heat so that the smoke from these facilities would not add to the air pollution. Factories and stores would likewise be closed.

New York was lucky that day because, fortunately, the mass of poisoned air passed. New Yorkers got off easy—they had a lucky escape that time. But the problem of polluted air has grown so serious for the big cities of the nation that we can no longer rely upon mere luck to save us.

And if the air we breathe is close to being poisonous, the water we drink is often not much better. "Every time you take a glass of water from a faucet in St. Louis, you are drinking from every flushed toilet from here to Minnesota."[1] These words by a newspaper editor may well be echoed by the people of most other cities as well. President Kennedy told Congress, "Pollution of our country's rivers and streams . . . has reached alarming proportions."[2] While the problem of clean air and water is almost universal, it is a particular problem for all big cities. Foul air and water seem to be a price that cities have paid for their progress, growth, and prosperity.

But how do air and water become polluted in the first place? If they are polluted, how bad is it? If it is bad, how can pollution be corrected—that is, how can the air we breathe and the water we drink be made and kept clean? If it is possible to keep air and water clean, how much will it cost and who is to pay the bill? If the bill can be paid, will the necessary steps to clean the air and the water be taken in time? These are very serious questions indeed, for our health and our very lives are dependent upon finding effective answers to the problems of air and water pollution.

Why Do We Have Dirty Air?

We have dirty air because we are alive. Our very breath is a pollutant, but we are saved by the fact that air has the ability to clean itself. Within limits,

'It's getting so bad that even people are complaining.'

(Mauldin, Chicago Sun-Times)

Industry's disregard of pollution prevention has caused countless situations like the one shown in this picture. Both public and private business has turned once pure waters like the Potomac into sewage pits. (Fred Ward, Black Star)

In addition to industrial pollution, city dwellers are bombarded with a wide variety of noxious gases escaping from buses, automobiles, incinerators, and trucks. (Claus C. Meyer, Black Star)

the air around us can absorb the pollutants (dirt
and dust and smoke) that are fed into it and get
rid of them in such a way that they are not harmful
to us. We are, therefore, safe as long as we do not
release more pollutants into the air than can be dis-
posed of by it. If proper balance is kept, we have
little to fear. It is when this balance is not maintained that our worries begin.

Man's worry over air pollution is not a new problem. It may be said to have begun when he was
born. It grew worse when man developed fire which
gave off smoke. Who would believe that the ancient
Romans complained because soot smudged their
wool togas? Or that England's King Edward I, during the Middle Ages, had a man put to death for
burning coal instead of oak? When Cortez and his
men traveled west, they saw a haze above what is
now the city of Los Angeles; Indians had built their
campfires. There, too, was polluted air.

It was not until relatively recent times, however,
that the problem of air pollution became serious. In
a certain sense it is the price we have paid for progress. This progress has taken the form of large factories that employ many people and produce the
necessities of life. The large cities in which we live
seem to intensify the problem of air pollution. The
incinerators in which we burn our garbage foul the
air. The exhaust from our cars and buses makes
the air unpleasant to breathe. The chimney soot and
smoke from the furnaces that heat our houses and
produce electricity make the air we breathe a danger
to health. The chemical waste given off by our most
modern factories has added new dangers to the
problem of air pollution.

The greatest cause of air pollution is the release
of unburned fuel into the air, usually in the form of

smoke or exhaust. Our fuels do not burn completely and therefore a percentage of unburned fuel is released as exhaust. Consider the fact that we depend on fire for nearly all our modern conveniences. A car, for example, runs by fire. There are a number of cylinders in the engine. In each cylinder is a piston. A carefully timed system allows the cylinders to fill with gasoline and air. When a cylinder is filled, a spark plug at the top of it causes the gasoline to explode and burn. The force of this explosion pushes the piston down and causes the car to move. But the gasoline does not burn completely; much of it escapes through the exhaust system and into the air as carbon monoxide—a deadly killer. "You've got a tiger in your tank, all right," one expert said, "but it's doing the work of a kitten."[3]

The automatic heating systems in houses, schools, office buildings, and apartments may have fancy controls and devices, but at the heart of them is fire. And if that fire uses gas, oil, or coal as fuel, it releases poison gases into the air. The incinerators in which our garbage is burned, the generators that produce our electricity, the factories that manufacture our goods all use fire as the basis of their operations, and all this fire releases pollutants into the air.

Smoke, odors, dust, fumes, all dirty the air we breathe. Garbage is picked up from the city streets, but, when burned in the cities' incinerators, it adds to the dirt in the air. Industry makes the necessities and luxuries of life, but the smoke from factories makes the air unbreathable. The plants that convert petroleum into gasoline give forth a smoke that is so filled with acid that it makes one's eyes smart and throat burn. The jet planes that can take us within hours to any place on the globe give forth a poisonous odor from jet fuel that pervades every

At present 60.6 percent of air pollution comes from cars. A recent government panel concluded that electrical battery powered cars are not the answer to the problem. Instead, they urged controls on the use of lead in gasoline and stressed the need for more electrically powered mass transit facilities. (Washington [D. C.] Evening Star)

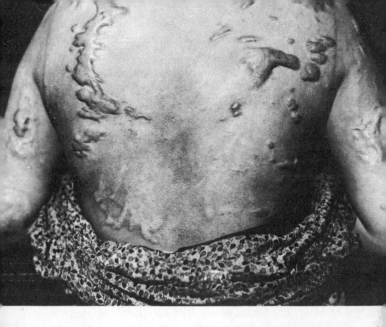

A survivor of the Hiroshima atomic bomb explosion retains scars. (Wide World)

major airport in the land. It is little wonder that, although more airports are desperately needed, few cities wish to have them as neighbors. And the chemicals we use to kill the insects that are believed to be destroying our crops may also have the incidental effect of destroying our lungs as well.

Probably the greatest possible danger in the air we breathe is the so-called fallout of radioactive materials from an atomic fission bomb. Indeed, in a world which sits on a growing stockpile of bombs, the direct destruction from the explosion—immeasurably great though it would be—would probably not be as great as the indirect destruction of life from poisoned air. The limitation on above-ground testing of nuclear weapons was largely necessary for fear that in the very process of manufacturing greater weapons and testing them, we were poisoning the air beyond the limits of safety.

When Is Air a Killer?

On a clear, windy day the air can rid itself of great amounts of pollutants. On these brisk days the smoke, soot, chemicals given off by homes, cars, buses, and factories are absorbed into the air and are briskly blown away. But during those periods when the smoke, soot, and chemicals are not blown away but hang over the city, the air we breathe becomes dangerous to our health. Many of the great cities of the world, including New York, London, Los Angeles, and Tokyo, live constantly within the shadow of death brought on by polluted air.

"In December 1930, a thick and stagnant fog enveloped a heavily industrialized section of Meuse Valley, Belgium. By the third day, many persons developed throat irritation, hoarseness, cough, and breathlessness. Some were nauseated. Some died. The elderly and those already ill with respiratory disease or heart disease were most vulnerable."[4]

Twenty people died and thousands became sick in Donora, Pennsylvania in 1948. When a fog covered the area, its effects were felt for years. "Ten years later, death and sickness rates in Donora, Pennsylvania were much higher for people who had become sick from the fog than for those who hadn't."[5]

In 1952 a fog settled over the city of London, England. For a period of two weeks the dirt and soot that were released into the air by the city were trapped. They could not escape. During those two weeks, the death rate in London rose 4,000 to 5,000 above the average.

These incidents are dramatic, but doctors are also concerned with the ordinary pollution that is a constant part of the air we breathe. This is the kind of pollution that makes breathing more difficult for people with asthma or allergies. This is the kind of pollution that makes the incidence of lung cancer much higher in the cities than elsewhere. Foul air irritates the eyes and contributes to eye disease. It brings on hoarseness of the throat and voice. It makes for a "runny" nose and may bring on excessive sneezing and coughing. While air pollution takes its toll in deaths, it also takes a toll in earnings that are lost through illness. It may make some invalids and may force others to remain in bed. In short, air pollution not only may destroy the health of men but also may deny to the rest of us the contributions of those people to our comfort, safety, and welfare.

While smoke and soot trapped in a layer of stagnant air may cause death as they did in Donora, in London, and in many other cities, smoke and tars inhaled directly into the lungs by cigarette smoking likewise contribute to illness and death. Evidence appears to be mounting that just as lung ailments increase as a result of poisoned air, so too, such sicknesses appear to increase with the smoke we inhale directly when smoking. The campaign against smoking urged by the Surgeon General of the United States and the campaign for cleaner air may be viewed as part of the overall problem of safeguarding the nation's health. While one obviously cannot stop breathing even foul and poisoned air, it is equally obvious that one can at least stop smok-

Travelers on major highways are often victims of accidents during heavy fog conditions caused by wastes from nearby industrial plants. (Gene Daniels, Black Star)

ing and thus not add to those factors that can make for illness.

There are indirect hazards to health from smog (fog and poisoned air) as well as direct ones. The smog cuts visibility. Traffic delays and accidents and often injuries are among the results. It is difficult, if not impossible, to determine the exact degree to which smog contributed to each accident in which someone was hurt. And yet, the smog that hangs over most major cities from time to time is regarded as a leading cause of accidents. The New Jersey

Turnpike was "blacked out" by fog and air pollution 23 times in 1965, and on that highway, bordering as it does chemical plants which give off acid-filled fumes, the accident rate has been consistently high. Similarly, a study made by the Civil Aeronautics Board listed "obstructions to vision" in the air by smoke, haze, sand, and dust as a major factor contributing to aircraft accidents. Ships in harbors and along the coasts suffer from similar problems.

What Is the Financial Cost of Air Pollution?

It is just as difficult to figure out the dollar costs of air pollution as it is to determine the medical costs. In a study made in 1960 it was found that air pollution may cost the so-called average family as much as $200 per person per year, or $800 per "typical" family of four. "This air tax is made in many different ways, some obvious and some amazingly subtle. Buildings, clothing, tires, metals, plants, virtually every kind of property is attacked by polluted air."[6] The household bills to clean curtains, drapes, rugs, upholstery, and laundry are a staggering economic cost, a cost often not obvious or realized. Such costs represent a "hidden" tax for all of us.

The cost of air pollution is paid for in the food we buy. Plants are probably more sensitive to dirty air than are human beings. And farms even miles away from the cities suffer great damage from air pollution. Farm losses in California are believed to be around $100 million per year. These losses are inevitably passed on to the consumer in the form of higher food prices. "It is believed that the air is so dirty in parts of New York, New Jersey, Florida,

California, Oregon, and Washington, that the crop damage from pollution now costs farmers more than the combined havoc of wind, cold, and ice. And much of this cost is passed on to the consumers."[7]

Other costs must be noted as well:

Trees near bus stops where they are exposed to excessive amounts of diesel fumes are likely to lose their leaves prematurely.

The evaporation of gasoline from automobiles costs the owners about $3 billion per year.

The sulfur that goes up the chimneys of power plants and factories is worth at least $300 million per year.[8]

In short, not only is air pollution a menace to health and costly in a thousand obvious and hidden ways, but the pollutants themselves represent wastes of our resources that we can ill afford. If such wastes could be recaptured or reused more efficiently, we would be accomplishing a great deal indeed. In the first place, we would have cleaner air. In the second place, we would be conserving desperately needed natural resources in the form of coal, oil, copper, water, chemicals, and fertile soil.

How Do We Poison Our Water?

The civilizations of ancient times owed their greatness to water. Ancient Egypt owed its greatness to the waters of the Nile, and ancient Babylonia to the waters of the Tigris and Euphrates Rivers. Ancient India owed its greatness to the waters of the Indus, and ancient China to the waters of the Yellow River.

It was upon the waters of lakes and rivers that the great cities of America grew. New York City owes its greatness to the waters of the Hudson, at whose mouth it is located. And Chicago, America's sec-

Port cities like Cleveland, Ohio, were one of the first areas to be faced with severe pollution problems. The filth seen here in the Cuyahoga River travels into Lake Erie which is now stagnant beyond redemption. (U.S. Department of the Interior)

ond city, owes its growth to its location on the waters of Lake Michigan. Pittsburgh, the nation's steel center, owes its prominence to its location at the point where the waters of the Allegheny and the Monongahela meet to form the mighty Ohio River. Cleveland rose to prominence because it is a port of entry on Lake Erie; while the site of the nation's capital, Washington, D.C., was chosen because of its location on the banks of the Potomac.

Today each of these waters is polluted. It is likely that if these lakes and rivers were in days past as filthy as they are today, great centers of civiliza-

This waterway in the Bronx is so ridden with garbage that its usefulness as a possible recreation site cannot be considered. Nevertheless, many city children deprived of more sanitary facilities often swim in places such as this. (Philip Gendreau)

tion would never have taken root and developed near them. The Potomac River has been described as "an open cesspool."[9] "Lake Erie is literally turning into a dead sea. This huge body of water, reaching from Buffalo at its eastern tip to Toledo at its western, is being reduced to a foul sewer for manmade garbage."[10] The Hudson, too, is so polluted that much of it can no longer be relied upon to furnish water to the cities which draw upon it.

The sewers which our waterways have become have been made by man. Just as the air has a substantial ability to clean itself by blowing away dust and smoke, so, too, can a swiftly running river or lake cleanse itself of a reasonable deposit of sewage, plant, animal, human, and industrial waste. Water can dissolve or break up wastes emptied into it. The chemicals it absorbs become valuable in making plants grow and in making the earth fertile. But when the amount of waste dumped into a waterway becomes too high, that waterway becomes polluted. It becomes unfit for drinking. It is not usable in industry. It cannot be used to water plants or irrigate fields. Fish living in the water die. Odors develop that make the shores unfit to live upon. Recreation opportunities, such as swimming and fishing, decline or disappear. Since a great deal of sewage finds its way to the coast, many once-beautiful beaches have been designated "unfit for swimming." Water shortages develop, shortages that are touched off by a relatively small drop in the normal amount of rainfall.

City sewage and waste from mine and factory may be regarded as the chief causes of water pollution. A lesser cause, but a growing and important one, is the pollution created by chemicals used to kill insects and fertilize crops. The water, polluted by these chemicals, finds its way into our lakes and rivers—bodies of water upon which we rely for drinking, washing, and industrial use. Increasingly, radioactive wastes from factories working with uranium have become a considerable cause of water pollution. Rivers not polluted before, such as the Colorado, run the risk of becoming unusable because of radioactive contamination. How to rid the water of radioactive wastes has become a great and growing problem.

Intensifying the problem of water pollution is the fact that pollutants are absorbed into the beds of lakes and rivers. Groundwater, as this is called, is absorbed into the earth where it disappears from sight. It may have no odor and its pollution may be otherwise undetectable. But when polluted, it is a great danger. For one thing, polluted groundwater cannot be treated; it remains forever a potential poison to the water we use. For another, groundwater does not merely settle to the bottom of the lake or riverbed; instead, it moves, slowly and stealthily, often to rear its head once again in an entirely different place, rising into a new stream and poisoning that as well. Since all water at one time or another becomes groundwater, pollution of this "underground sea," as Rachel Carson calls it, is, in reality, "pollution of water everywhere."[11]

What Are the Dangers from Polluted Waters?

The danger from polluted water is twofold. On the one hand there is a danger to health. Polluted water may cause illness in stomach, intestines, nose, mouth, or eyes. Cholera, a still-dreaded disease in Asia and India, may be traced to impure water. While cholera no longer appears to be a dan-

This giant mechanical "clarifier" is part of a $2.5 million pollution control system at Kimberly-Clark's newsprint plant in Alabama. Process removes up to 98% of insoluble materials before water is returned to the Coosa River. (Wide World)

31

ger in the United States, other diseases are still traceable to polluted water. Infectious hepatitis, a disease of the liver, appears to be growing in this country. There seems to be mounting evidence that polluted water may be a contributing cause. Polio too has been at least partially traced to polluted water. And, depending upon the chemical content of the pollutant, there is some evidence that water pollution may lead to cancer. While we know that there is a significant relationship between polluted water and certain illnesses, we are not exactly sure what that relationship really is. Because we are uncertain, taking steps to minimize the effects of polluted water upon our health is a difficult project.

The second great danger from polluted water is that we will not have all the water our cities need to exist and to prosper. As cities grow, as standards of living rise, the amount of water we need likewise increases dramatically.

"About three gallons of water are used every time a toilet is flushed. . . . About 30 gallons of water are used to fill a bathtub to a depth of six inches. . . . A commercial air conditioner of the type ordinarily found in a restaurant or cafeteria uses enough water to supply the daily needs of about 30,000 people."[12]

It is estimated that "an urban family uses about six times as much water as a farm family that draws its water from a well."[13] When the growing number of dishwashers and clothes washers are added, one can easily see the increasing pressure upon the existing water supply and the ever greater need for pure, fresh water. The amount of water needed in industry and on farms will grow even

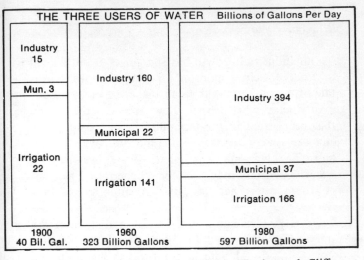

THE THREE USERS OF WATER — Billions of Gallons Per Day

1900	1960	1980
40 Bil. Gal.	323 Billion Gallons	597 Billion Gallons

1900: Industry 15; Mun. 3; Irrigation 22

1960: Industry 160; Municipal 22; Irrigation 141

1980: Industry 394; Municipal 37; Irrigation 166

Lewis Herber, *Crisis in Our Cities* (Englewood Cliffs, N.J.: Prentice-Hall, Inc., 1965), p. 93, used by permission.

1. How do our water requirements today differ from what they were in 1900? How do you account for this?
2. What is expected to happen to our water requirements by 1980? How do you account for this?
3. What are some of the uses of water in industry?
4. Why are irrigation needs growing?
5. In your judgment are we likely to have enough water to meet the needs of the 1980's? Why or why not?

more dramatically during the next decades. Because so much of our water has become unfit for use, a real question exists as to whether the cities of the nation will have all the water they really need. And since the greatest use of water is in industry, the problem really is whether enough water will be available to meet the needs of industrial growth.

Why Have We Failed?

Our industrial growth has sometimes been likened to Frankenstein's monster. If you have read this tale of horror, you will recall that it involves a German doctor who learned how to make the object that he created in the laboratory come to life. The monster that was created in time destroys the creator. The man-made polluted air we breathe and water we drink may well be likened to Frankenstein's monster, because, like the monster, it may destroy us.

On the other hand, you may also remember the story of Aladdin and his wonderful lamp. In this story, the boy Aladdin had but to rub his lamp and his every wish came true. In our society we must do more than rub a lamp for our wishes to come true. Yet, because of our skill in science and technology, we do have at our fingertips, as did Aladdin, the means by which our wishes can come true. In short, if we wish to have clean, pure, fresh air and water, we have the means and, in general, the know-how to bring this about. "We can handle just about any pollution-control demand that is likely to be made," says a manufacturer of devices that can keep our air and water clean and pure.[14] Yet despite the fact that we know how, strangely enough it appears that we do not really wish to have either clean air or pure water. Why?

For one thing, the costs of providing for either clean air or pure water are very high. At the present time it is estimated that $5 billion a year are being spent by industry and government in an effort to clean our air and water.[15] This figure is expected to double in three years. There are some who believe that to keep our air clean and water pure the generation reading this book may have to spend "up to $3,000 billion [three trillion dollars] for sewage and industrial waste treatment, automobile-exhaust control, incinerator improvement. . . ."[16] The problem here is not only the high costs involved, but who is to pay the bill?

On the one hand, each person contributes to air and water pollution. As a result, is it unfair to expect the public to pay the bill through higher taxes? On the other hand, industry is guilty on a massive scale of emptying factory wastes into the air we breathe and water we drink. Under these circumstances, is it too much to expect industry to pay the cost? But if these costs mount, as they will, can they be absorbed by industry indefinitely? The answer is, probably not. Should they be passed on through increased prices to the consumer? Such costs probably will be passed on to the consumer, but when the costs appear to be burdensome will the consumer continue to be willing to pay? Since the consumer may resist additional costs in the form of higher prices, should the government help finance industry's share by paying for at least a part of these costs? The author of an article in *Fortune,* a magazine devoted to the interests of industrial giants, feels that industry should be able to pay the costs for pure air and water and that for the most part the added cost to the consumer will not be very high. "The role of the Federal government . . . can largely be confined to setting standards, and to aiding state and local government in enforcement."[17]

But even here the problem has been who is responsible for pure air and fresh water in the first place? Although air and water pollution are national problems, there has been, as yet, but a feeble national attack on these problems. Instead, local laws of villages, towns, cities, and states have attempted to solve problems of air and water pollution. Thus, laws preventing the burning of fall leaves exist in some communities and not in others. In some communities the method of burning city rubbish is far more efficient than in others. Some states try to purify their water in one way and some in another. In some cities there is a separate water tax; in others none exists. In some cities water is metered, that is, the user pays only for the water he uses. In others, as in New York City, there is no metering of water. The result of city, state, and

In Tokyo, local authorities try to put teeth into smog control regulations. School children wear masks as protection against the rising incidence of respiratory ailments attributed to smog. (Wide World)

national interests in clean air and water has been
an abundance of laws. But these laws have often
been ineffective. They have often overlapped. Still
more often they could not be, or would not be, enforced.

Aggravating this problem is the fact that many
rivers are interstate in nature; that is, they run into
two or more states or are shared by them. The
Hudson, for example, is shared by New York and
New Jersey. Who is to pay the enormous cost of
keeping the Hudson clean? And who owns the air
above the cities and states in which smoke, soot,
and dirt originate? While New York City has a very
poor reputation for the cleanliness of its air, what
can New York do to improve it when a substantial
amount of the dirt in the air is actually produced
by the chemical factories that lie across the Hudson in the state of New Jersey, but within commut-
ing distance of New York? Obviously, this poses a
predicament which, while not so difficult that it cannot be solved, adds to the problem of cleaning
our air and water and helps partially to explain
why we have not been successful up to now in doing
so.

Contributing to the problem of providing clean
air and water has been the reluctance of industry
to make changes. The automobile industry, for example, has only grudgingly agreed to provide cars
with a so-called blow-by device to prevent the exhaust from cars from fouling our air. The importance of such a device was dramatically illustrated
in an article in *The New York Times* of October
14, 1967 which bore the following headline, "Auto
Fumes Force 40 Minute Closing of First Avenue
Tunnel."[18] It is not beyond the realm of possibility
that auto fumes that can kill may one day poison

In Omaha, Nebraska, waste from a meat packing plant spills out into an adjoining waterway. Blood, manure, and grease stain the water a red-brown color. (U.S. Department of the Interior)

the air of an entire city if that city continues to grow and the number of cars in use grows with it. Yet the industry has not been willing until recently to furnish the necessary device that would prevent such a disaster from overtaking us.

The electric utilities have been slow to change to fuels that would lessen the poisons given off into the air. Again, although they are beginning to change to higher-grade fuels which would give off less sulphur into the air, they do so only in the face of compulsion, public opinion, and public pressure. The detergents that the soap industry sells to housewives for "whiter wash," are emptied from the washer in the basement into the sewage system of the city and from thence into the streams and rivers of the nation. There they resist efforts to make them harmless. Industry has been slow either to find a detergent that could be made harmless with existing methods, or to find new methods. And because there was no united front by city, state, and nation, the industrial polluters were able to divide and conquer. Thus, if one city was about to pass a law to prevent the dumping of factory waste into the city's river, the factory would threaten to move. If it was the only factory giving employment to many, this threat was a serious one indeed. Too often, up to now, the needed law was never passed.

What Can Be Done?

There are many things that can be done by the individual, by industry, and by government to stop the further poisoning of our air and water.

WHAT THE INDIVIDUAL CAN DO:

1. Each individual can be alert to the need to have clean air and pure water. Toward this end, he needs to inform himself of what his city and state are doing to pass laws to prevent air and water pollution. He must be willing to vote for those people and for those laws that appear to offer the best possibilities of doing something about the problem. And he must be willing to bear at least some of the cost himself either in the taxes he pays or in the higher prices he pays.

2. Each individual must observe as carefully as he can the laws relating to air and water pollution. Thus, if the law requires, he must refrain from burning leaves. If he uses an incinerator, he must

be sure that it conforms at least to the minimum standards required by local law. In the case of water pollution, note should be taken of the effects of detergents upon the local availability of drinking water. Should he and his neighbors fail to do so, they may find that they will be drinking tomorrow the soapsuds they created yesterday.

3. To the extent possible, drivers should keep their automobiles in efficient running condition. This will mean the more efficient use of gasoline, a greater number of miles to the gallon of gasoline, and the more economical operation of the automobile. And, above all, it will mean that a minimum amount of exhaust will be discharged into the air.

WHAT INDUSTRY CAN DO:

1. Industry can develop improved methods of manufacture that would have the dual effect of using profitably products now wasted and also of minimizing the number of pollutants given off into the air and water. It should be willing to use higher grades of raw materials which, upon burning, will give off less smoke or other pollutants into the air.

2. Industry should be ready to adopt any and all devices that will help reduce, if not eliminate, air and water pollution. Often, the desire to save money makes industry slow to take the steps that are needed to buy or make those instruments that can curb pollution. It is probably not an overstatement to say that every kind of pollution could be corrected if industry would speedily make the necessary investment.

3. Industry should observe the laws that exist against pollution. Often, industry has avoided or evaded the law. When caught it has cheerfully

Tomorrow morning when you get up, take a nice deep breath. It'll make you feel rotten.

Every day your lungs breathe in air that contains sulfur dioxide (which contributes to chronic bronchitis and pulmonary emphysema), benzopyrene (which has produced cancer on the skin of mice), carbon monoxide (which, in sufficient quantities, will kill you), acrolein (which was an ingredient in tear gas in World War I) and enough soot and dirt to turn your lungs black, instead of the healthy pink they're supposed to be.

No wonder you feel lousy.

If these facts bother you, send your name and address to: Citizens for Clean Air, Inc., Box One Million, Grand Central Station N.Y. 10017.

When storm sewers and sanitation sewers are combined, untreated sewage may be dumped into nearby streams when there is a heavy storm. (Charles Steinacker, Black Star)

paid the fines imposed by a court, in the full knowledge that paying the fines was probably cheaper than observing the law in the first place or taking needed corrective measures. This preference for paying the penalty rather than obeying the law is a disservice to the city and the state in which the industry is located and is a menace to the health of the people.

WHAT CITIES AND STATES CAN DO:

1. Cities and states can pass appropriate laws making illegal the pollution of air or water. The laws should contain strong penalties including not only fines, but jail sentences for the owners or responsible officers of the industry found guilty of fouling the air or water.

2. Since states often share problems of water and air pollution, they should take steps to work together by forming bi-(two) or tri-(three) state authorities with the power to deal expressly with common problems of air and water pollution.

3. Cities in particular must improve the methods they use to burn or otherwise get rid of rubbish. Too often, the city that urges industry to find means of reducing air and water pollution is itself contributing to pollution. Sometimes it dumps city garbage into rivers and streams and near bathing beaches. Sometimes it fails to keep its incinerators in good repair. As a result, the garbage it burns gives off more smoke than is necessary. In this way, the city is often as guilty as industry of contributing to polluted air.

4. Each city needs to develop efficient means of purifying its water supply. It must modernize existing facilities. Many cities make the mistake of

combining storm sewers and sanitation sewers. Storm sewers are designed to prevent flooding after a rainfall or heavy storm. Sanitation sewers are designed to drain off sewage into a sewage treatment plant where chemicals break down the waste before it is released into a stream or ocean. When such sewers are combined, a heavy storm produces a volume of water that proves too much for the sewage treatment plant. The result is that a great amount of untreated sewage, including animal and human solid waste, is dumped untreated into the nearby streams.

5. Cities should take advantage of federal assistance in the form of grants to improve their facilities. They should also try to maintain standards of quality in waters within their boundaries. This is now a requirement passed by Congress in the Water Quality Control Act of 1965. In New York State, 1972 is the date by which all of the state's waters will be pure if the goals of the current Pure Waters Program are achieved. But this is a dream only. It remains to be seen whether performance will equal promise.

WHAT THE FEDERAL GOVERNMENT CAN DO:

1. The federal government must take a more active interest in air and water pollution than ever before. Since these are national problems, they must be met with the strong arm of the national government. This requires Congress to enforce old laws and to pass new ones. It requires power to act against polluters.

2. The federal government must appropriate funds to help cities and states improve their sewage facilities. Laws authorizing such appropriations have

already been passed. Cities and states, however, have not been quick to take advantage of the generosity of the federal government since often the law requires the cities and states to put up a portion of the cost before the federal government supplies the rest.

3. The federal government might help industry directly to devise new methods of eliminating pollution. It might help industry by paying costs of basic pollution research. It might help by paying part of the expense of the change-overs that will be required if new methods of manufacture are adopted.

Increasingly, private citizens, industry, and government have become aware of the need to "do something" about air and water pollution. Conscious of the mounting concern, one major electric company has been broadcasting the following TV commercial to describe its effort to make New York City's air cleaner:

When the air in New York is dirty,
When pollution is causing a fuss,
Most people see red
And think of Con Ed,
And they point a finger at us.
But . . .
When the air in New York is balmy,
When the air in New York is nice,
People look at the sky
And they hurry on by—
They don't think of Con Edison twice.

(Voice only): It's only human nature. Every time a puff of smoke comes out of a Con Edison stack, people seem to know about it. But they *don't* know all the ways Con Ed is working to help clean up

New York's air. With electrostatic ash catchers.*
With combustion-controls.* And, in October we'll
be using a special low-sulphur fuel oil.

> We're working to make New York cleaner,
> Better than ever before,
> So don't ask if we care about cleaning up air,
> Con Edison couldn't care more.[19]

But is a jingle enough? Are any of us doing
enough? Can we do more? How? And can we
do more in time to make our air and water pure for
those living today? Will New York's promise to
have all its water pure by 1972 be kept? Can it
be kept? Will other states do as well in water and air
purification programs? These are questions that cannot be answered today. But what is done today will
determine whether we will have clean air and water tomorrow.

---

electrostatic ash catchers—electric attraction screens
which filter smoke coming from a chimney.

combustion-controls—prevent fires from burning too
hotly.

Part Two
Selected
Readings

The air we breathe may well be described as a witches' brew of dust, dirt,
poisonous gases, and a host of unseen,
but foul-smelling pollutants. These pollutants hide the sun, dirty our clothes,
and make us ill. An unseen enemy is
often the most dangerous. Why are air
pollutants described as an unseen enemy?

1

There's Something
in the Air

by LUCY KAVALER

WHILE you sit quietly reading this article, you
are breathing at a rate of 14 to 18 times
a minute. Each time, you are inhaling air that
contains many things you never learned about in
school when studying the composition of the atmo-

From the August 1966 issue of *Redbook* Magazine, copyright ©
1966 by McCall Corporation. Reprinted by permission of Lucy
Kavaler. Copyright © 1966 by Lucy Kavaler.

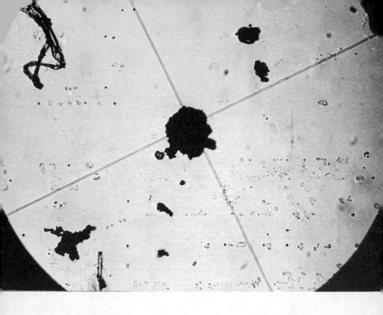

A view of the trash that floats about in the St. Louis County air, magnified forty times by a microscope. (St. Louis Post Dispatch from Black Star)

sphere. Each breath carries some 40,000 particles of dust if you are surrounded by "clean" country air, some 70,000 if you live in the city. Then come the noxious gases. The burning of coal for heat and power sends 48,000 tons of sulphur dioxide into the air every day. The nation's 88 million motor vehicles daily release 250,000 tons of carbon monoxide, 16,500 to 33,000 tons of hydrocarbons and 4,000 to 12,000 tons of nitrogen oxides. To this must be added a host of other fumes . . . by-products of the metallurgical, chemical, petroleum, and other industries.

Stir this unwholesome mixture well and it makes the air we have around us on a normal day. To turn this into a disaster situation requires only a windless day and a weather condition known scientifically as a thermal inversion, which means simply that the air is warm where it should be cold and vice versa. Warm air usually rises from near the ground to the cooler areas higher up. As it climbs it carries pollutants with it, and at least a portion of them are scattered into the upper air. Should the upper air become warm, however, it acts as a cover, and the cold, polluted air near the ground does not rise. This is what happened in London and in Donora.

Though the effects of pollution are seldom as devastating as during a disaster, they surround us every day. Look up at the gray sky where there should be sunshine. It is not really a cloudy day; high above the layer of smoke the sun is bright and the sky is blue. Dust the window sills in a city apartment and come back an hour or two later and they

Sulfur dioxide in the air caused these tulip plants to wither. (U.S. Public Health Service)

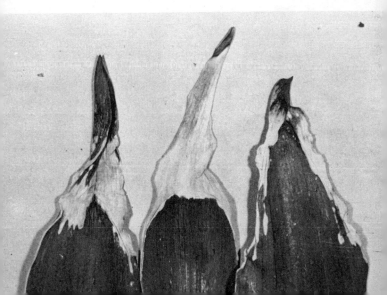

will be covered with soot. Leave the car out over-night and a fine layer of dust will dull its finish. The clothes hanging on the line are often gray by the time you take them down, no matter how carefully you washed them. Glance out the window at the columns of smoke rising from nearby power plants, factories or apartment-house incinerators.

And this is just the pollution you can see. The unseen pollutants—the colorless, sometimes odorless gases—are worse by far. The clear cold air of winter is merely an illusion; pollution often reaches its

Smog engulfs cities throughout the country. This photograph was taken of St. Louis in the middle of the day. (St. Louis Post Dispatch)

highest levels when fuel is burned to heat our homes and industrial production is in full swing.

There is no place to hide from these menaces. The United States Public Health Service reports that any community that has a population of 50,000 or more has a real problem. Not only Los Angeles, New York and Chicago, but also Denver, Phoenix and Las Vegas are among the more than 300 cities engulfed in major air pollution. And those countless Americans who moved to the suburbs for a cleaner, healthier life are only slightly better off than their city friends.

"The effects of air pollution," says Vernon G. MacKenzie, chief of the Division of Air Pollution of the U.S. Department of Health, Education and Welfare, "are directly experienced by the more than half of our population living in our great widespread urban-suburban complexes."

FURTHER INQUIRY

1. Why is an "air inversion" a health hazard?
2. Is air pollution likely to be greater in winter or summer? Why?
3. Is there any "escape" from air pollution?
4. Why are unseen pollutants likely to be worse than the ones we see?
5. Why are people in the suburbs only slightly better off?

Today, polluted air threatens the
health of most Americans. As this selection shows, dirty air is not confined
to large cities alone. Now the problem
of air pollution has spread to places
where it had never been before. How do
you account for the spread of air pollution? Why is there no place to hide?

2

No Place to Hide

by BEN H. BAGDIKIAN

A T one o'clock in the morning about a month ago,
Peter Briola, a tough and spirited lawyer, sat
up in bed with a familiar agony. He was alone in his
white clapboard house in Lincoln, a town of 3,600
people in the middle of Maine. The typical New

From "Death in Our Air" by Ben H. Bagdikian, *Saturday
Evening Post*, October 8, 1966. Copyright © 1966 by Curtis Pub-
lishing Company. Reprinted by permission of the author's
agent, The Sterling Lord Agency, Inc.

Ernie Bushmiller, United Feature Syndicate

England homestead . . . looks like a romantic painting of an idyllic scene of peace and purity, of an unspoiled America.

"It was like all the other times, as though someone had you by the throat, trying to choke you. There was that terrible smell, like rotting dead stuff. You begin to cough and gasp. Your eyes run. You shut the windows, but it doesn't do any good. Nothing does any good."

Here among the ancient spruce of the deep woods, a paper mill is pouring filth upon Peter

55

Briola and his fellow townsmen. They suffer from a contamination that has now infested every city in the United States and not a few small towns. Today, polluted air threatens the health of most Americans, corrodes* their property, obscures or obliterates their scenery and insults their peace of mind. Unclean air is no longer rare in American cities. It is the rule.

City and country, voices are rising to protest. Norman Cousins, editor of the *Saturday Review,* and chairman of a New York City task force on air pollution, recently concluded: "More poisons are pumped into the air in New York than anywhere else in the United States." Yet, Ed Christopherson, a writer who left Manhattan for Missoula, Montana, "Garden Spot of the West," found there was no place to hide. "When I lived in New York," he says, "I used to watch the clinkers come down the airshaft and remember how great the pine-scented evening downdrafts smelled in Missoula, and this was an important factor in my moving out here. Today Missoula is the country's second worst smog area." As a counter to the state's Big Sky Country booster slogan, some Missoulans are posting signs out on the highways saying, "Missoula, Montana— Dirty Sky Country."

Mrs. Peter Rose, a housewife on a major thoroughfare in Denver, "The Mile-High City," says: "Twenty years ago when we moved into this bungalow it was a delight. The yard had nice green grass and beautiful roses. The whole neighborhood was clean. The house needed only one good cleaning a week, and the curtains and drapes I used to clean twice a year. From the neighborhood you could see

———

corrodes—rusts.

the mountains clearly most of the time, with snow-caps visible through that wonderful purple. But in the last few years, since they made the road one-way and started the traffic growing the way it has —well, about six years ago my husband began having eye trouble, irritation and watering. A short time later my eyes did the same thing. We both began getting frequent inflammations like sinus trouble. The doctor has us use eyewashes every day now. The roses all shriveled and died. The lawn began to go. Half the time you can't see the mountains anymore. I have to clean the house every day, and it's still gritty and greasy. Curtains and drapes can stand cleaning every week. I've got forty-five windows in the house, and they need a cleaning every week instead of twice a year. It's the same house and the neighborhood is still a nice residential one, but the air has become dirty, uncomfortable and expensive."

Dr. La Rele Stephens, a physician in Moscow, Idaho, says he can almost tell by the barometer and the direction of the wind when he will begin getting calls from patients in Lewiston, a town of 13,000 that is 29 miles away: "When the wind blows the mill fumes over the town or there is a dead calm, the patients begin to come in with respiratory troubles, nasal congestion, allergies, difficulty in breathing, lots of sneezing. I'm convinced we get some deaths, too, because when the fumes make natural fogs thicker, which you can tell by the smell, we get more automobile accidents."

Donald McLean, of Polk County, Florida, told a Senate committee that since phosphate plants began putting seven tons of fluorides a day into the air he has had to sell his cattle and his citrus groves because the cattle sickened and died, crops that

A cow suffering from a bone disease caused by fluoride poisoning. Note bone damage to the skeleton. In extreme cases animals cannot tolerate the anguish of standing. (Robertson Studios)

used to mature in 80 days now take 200, barbed wire that used to last 20 years rots in 4, and he doesn't dare grow vegetables for his family for fear they will pick up the same chemicals that fall onto his pastures and groves. "It eats up the paint and etches glass, it kills trees, it kills cattle. It is an irritant to mucous membrane, and we have sore throats, tears run out of our eyes, we sneeze, we have nosebleeds. Gentlemen, am I a fool to assume that that stuff [is] injurious to humans?"

There is evidence that Mr. McLean is no fool.

Danger to health and property from unclean air is increasing. Some places, like Lincoln, Maine, and Polk County, Florida have special and dramatic problems. But every American city of more than 50,000 population has air pollution serious enough to worry about. . . .

FURTHER INQUIRY

1. How do you think people employed by an industry react to contamination caused by that industry? Do you think they complain? Do you think they would organize protest groups?
2. How do you think politicians, congressmen, senators, mayors respond to the problem?

Here the author maintains that New York is a city destroying itself because of its foul air and water. Why does the author say that New Yorkers have been neglectful?

3

A City Destroying Itself

by RICHARD J. WHALEN

New York's Dirty Air

THE foul air of New York, dirtier than that of any other major city, threatens public health and costs the citizens an estimated $520 million annually. Our dirty atmosphere is intolerable and could

From "*A City Destroying Itself: An Angry View of New York*" by Richard J. Whalen. Copyright © 1964, 1965 by Time, Inc. Reprinted by permission of William Morrow and Company, Inc.

Smokestacks and cars—this photographic negative emphasizes the sources of urban pollution. (The New York Times)

be cleansed by the enforcement of stringent laws. Yet we go on tolerating it. Nothing more neatly underscores the pathetic deprivations* of city life than the fact that private citizens, alarmed at official

pathetic deprivations—sad denials.

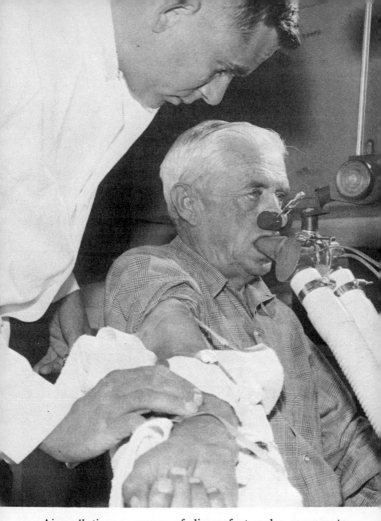

Air pollution, a source of discomfort and a menace to health, is either a cause or aggravating factor to a number of respiratory diseases, including lung cancer, emphysema, asthma, chronic bronchitis, and the common cold. (U.S. Public Health Service)

neglect of an essential public interest, found it necessary to organize a pressure group, Citizens for Clean Air, Inc. Soon afterward, a special committee of the City Council, headed by the able Councilman Robert A. Low, launched a study of air pollution. Its interim findings, released this summer, remind us that we are poisoning ourselves with every breath we take.

"It has been generally concluded," reports the Low Committee, "that air pollution is one of the factors contributing to the steady increase of lung cancer." A person breathing the city's air inhales as much benzopyrene, a cancer-inducing hydrocarbon, as he would if he smoked two packs of cigarettes a day. Dust particles can carry the benzopyrene to sensitive areas of the lungs—and there is no lack of dust in the city. On every square mile of New York, an average of 60 tons of heavy dust falls each month; in Manhattan, 80 tons. This is the filth that begrimes shirt collars and blackens windows; the deadly pollutants are the ones we cannot see— chiefly carbon monoxide, nitrogen dioxide, and sulphur dioxide.* The average level and the maximum level of sulphur dioxide recorded in New York are higher than in any other major U.S. city.

While the menace of air pollution to public health is plain, medical researchers, poring over statistical studies of the city's recurring smog episodes, are compelled to speak only of "excess deaths," mainly among infants and elderly persons. Some 170 "excess deaths" occurred in November, 1953, when a nine-day "temperature inversion" caused pollutants to

---

carbon monoxide . . . sulphur dioxide—chemicals in automobile exhausts, in factory and incinerator smoke.

accumulate in the air over the city. During a two-week period in early 1963, a combination of heavy air pollution, extreme cold, and an epidemic of Asian influenza is believed to have caused some 400 more deaths than normal in New York. If hundreds of people fell dead on the streets, action would come at once. But the figures on "excess deaths" come to public attention at the measured pace of scientific research, long after the fact, and so lose much of their impact. A do-nothing Mayor greets such figures with a statement piously cautioning against "incitement to fright and panic."

Observes a researcher who studies New York's atmosphere: "Air pollution exemplifies what happens in a chaotic situation. Everyone's lack of concern mixes in the air."

To provide the people with tolerably clean air is a prime responsibility of municipal government. But that huge, self-frustrating entity,* which officially opposes air pollution, also contributes mightily to it. Indeed, what the city negligently does to worsen air pollution, such as operating a fleet of 4,200 poorly maintained buses, makes a mockery of its official opposition. The city's Department of Air Pollution Control is a stepchild agency, with a budget of just over a million dollars a year, and an enforcement staff of only forty-five inspectors to cover 320 square miles. Ironically, much of the soot the city chases comes . . . from 12,000 apartment-house incinerators. In 1951 the Department of Sanitation, short of trucks and dumping grounds, lobbied through a municipal regulation requiring incinerators in new apartment houses four stories or higher. Burning garbage in an inefficient apartment-house

---

self-frustrating entity—in this case, the city itself.

incinerator reduces its bulk by as little as 25 per cent, an accommodation to the Sanitation Department for which New Yorkers pay a fantastic price. New York's uniquely bad sulphur dioxide pollution is the result of the city's complacently allowing large fuel oil users, such as factories, apartment houses, and Con Edison power plants (Con Edison is the largest user of all, burning half the city's fuel), to burn a cheap, sludgy grade of oil with a high sulphur content. Over the next few years, under a new fuel oil code, such users will have to substitute a somewhat better and "cleaner" grade of oil.

Thus does New York attack enormous problems with toothpicks.

New York's Dirty Water

The waters around New York are heavily polluted, the result of the shortsighted assumption over several generations that, regardless of what the city heedlessly did, it could not destroy so great a natural asset. The cumulative effect of popular and political indifference has been felt in recent generations. It was cheaper to lay one pipe to carry both sewage and storm water rather than two, so the city built combined sewers, which overflow treatment plants* following even a moderate rainfall.

As recently as 1935 the city did not have a single modern treatment plant, and it still does not have enough of them. They routinely pump raw sewage into the Hudson and East Rivers, more than a half-billion gallons daily, relying on what sanitary engineers vividly describe as "excellent flushes." As

---

treatment plant—installation that adds chemicals to change sewage into harmless substances.

a result of such disgusting "flushing" along much of the 150-mile course from Albany to New York, the mighty Hudson, "the great river of the mountains," has become a rank cesspool.

According to state studies, the river is six times more polluted then it was at the turn of the century while the state's population has increased less than two and a half times. The despoliation by preceding generations* denies ourselves and our children (and probably *their* children) a significant part of our natural heritage. Even if all forms of pollution were magically to cease tomorrow, the befouled Hudson could not cleanse itself, and be fit for swimming and fishing, until well into the next century. The end of pollution is not in sight.

FURTHER INQUIRY

1. To what extent can air and water pollution destroy a city?
2. What factors make New York's air and water so dirty?
3. How does the city itself contribute to its own pollution problems?
4. What is a pressure group? Is such a group good or bad? Why?
5. Why is it "false economizing" to use one pipe rather than two for storm water and sewage?

---

despoliation by preceding generations—spoiling by people who came before us.

In the book from which this selection is taken, the authors accuse us of not doing enough for clean air. Why is there much talk but little done about air pollution?

4

Indictment

by EDWARD EDELSON *and* FRED WARSHOFSKY

UNLESS you live in Los Angeles or Chicago, your city is not doing enough about air pollution.

Unless you live in California, your state's air-pollution-control law is inadequate for an effective program.

Unless you live in Chicago, Cincinnati, Detroit, Los Angeles, New York, Philadelphia, San Francisco or Washington, D.C., your local air-pollution officials probably do not even have accurate information on what is in the air.

After two decades of loud talk and cries of alarm, that is the discouraging picture of the fight against air pollution. The talk goes on, swelling to a crescendo at election time in most cities, but dropping to a whisper when budget hearings come around. The most discouraging fact is not merely that most communities are waging the battle against air pollution halfheartedly and more with words than with dollars. It is far more disheartening that despite long, detailed and clear statements by responsible officials about the nature and size of the air-pollution problem, most communities have not even laid the groundwork for an intelligent fight, and much money now spent for cleaner air is being wasted.

The logical priorities* for the campaign are clear: Find out how bad the problem is; search out the sources of pollution; then take the measures that will cost the least and will do the most good. By these standards, the anti-pollution fight generally is being waged on very illogical terms. Only where the problem has been shoved down the throats of local officials, have intelligent programs been forthcoming; smoke in Pittsburgh and St. Louis, photochemical smog in Los Angeles. That leaves only Chicago, of all the other cities in the United States, as a community that has moved against the problem of air pollution before it had become critical

------

logical priorities—most appropriate things to do in their order of importance.

The pollution problem cannot be overdramatized. (Specifying Engineer)

At an air monitoring station atop the Municipal Court Building in St. Louis, two Public Health engineers check lead "candle" which measures sulfur dioxide. (St. Louis Post Dispatch from Black Star)

and in full recognition of the intricate complexities of the campaign to be fought.

The typical city is faced neither with the eye-stinging photochemical smog that blinds Los Angeleans, nor with the sulphur-rich smoke that blotted out the sun in St. Louis and Pittsburgh. In most cities, smog is a mixture of both kinds of pollution, the exact nature of the mixture determined by the number and concentration of cars in the area, the type of industry in the city, and often the weather conditions and geography of the region. This makes it very hard to draw up a list of the ten most-polluted cities in the country. Of the first two

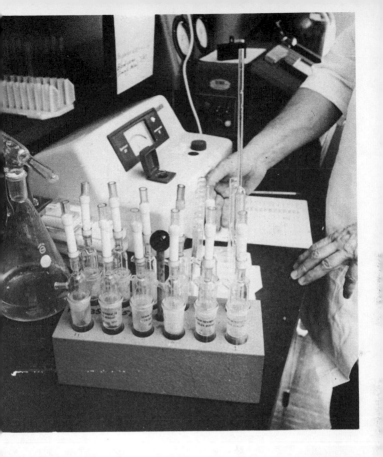

Concentrations of sulfur dioxide in the air at specific times of day can be determined with this gas sampler. Every two hours air is drawn through tubes containing chemicals which retain only the sulfur dioxide. (St. Louis Post Dispatch from Black Star)

places on such a list, however, there is little doubt. Los Angeles is conceded to have the worst air-pollution problem in the country, because of its special combination of weather, geography and population density. New York City is generally given second place. This is largely a tribute to its sheer size, since weather conditions in New York are not particularly conducive to air pollution and its industry is not of the smog-generating kind. Nevertheless, nearly a tenth of the nation's population is concentrated in the metropolitan New York area; millions of cars jam its streets; the industrial complex of northern New Jersey sends its fumes across the river—and almost as often the city returns in kind —and all of these factors add up to an air-pollution problem that would long since have reached the crisis stage if New York were not perched on the sea and fanned by brisk winds.

FURTHER INQUIRY

1. Is the accusation (indictment) fair for your city? For your state? Why, or why not?
2. Do you agree or disagree with the steps the author suggests are needed to have clean air?

The selection below is from the second of three articles which tell of the misfortunes that followed when a ship and its crew were subjected to radioactive fallout. Several of the crew died after a long and ugly illness, relations between the United States and Japan reached a new low, and the problem of controlling radioactivity from nuclear tests was sharply dramatized.

5

The Voyage of the Lucky Dragon

by RALPH E. LAPP

A T 5:30 A.M. on Sunday, March 14, 1954, the Japanese fishing vessel *Fukuryu Maru (Lucky Dragon)* No. 5 returned to its home port of Yaizu, some 120 miles south of Tokyo. Its crew had been fishing for tuna near the Marshall Islands and had seen the flash of an American atomic bomb test; shortly afterward a rain of white ash had fallen on

These victims suffered from burns after the atomic bomb struck Hiroshima. But for some survivors, the effects were even more disfiguring. (Wide World)

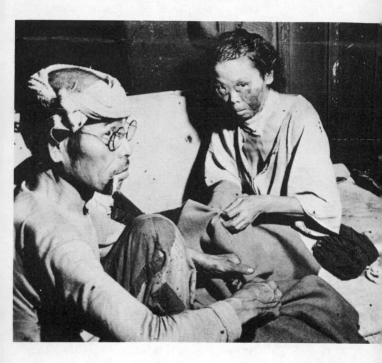

the ship. During their return trip the men had been listless and debilitated; some complained of burning eyes, itching skin, and nausea; others were losing their hair. The owner, Kakuichi Nishikawa, glanced at one of the sailors when the boat tied to the pier and noticed that he was terribly dark, as though deeply sunburned.

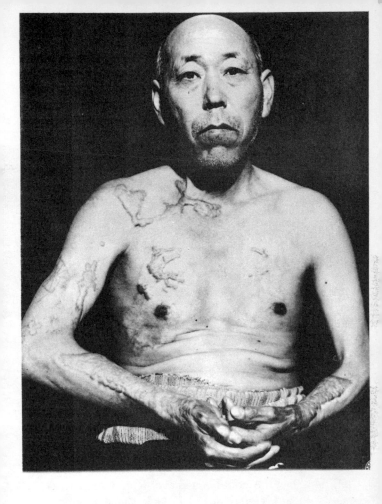

Nishikawa and Yoshio Misaki, the ship's Fishing Master, immediately called the Yaizu hospital, but it was Sunday and the woman who answered told Misaki that they could accept only emergency cases. It was not until he managed to locate Dr. Ooi, the doctor in charge, that Misaki could arrange for the men to come to the hospital at 1:00 P.M.

Dr. Ooi was a surgeon, who felt that routine physical checkups were not in his bailiwick, and at first
he could make no sense of the men's appearance.
Though their faces were dark, they seemed in good
spirits. Sanjiro Masuda, who looked the worst, was
severely burned on the face, ears, and lips, and
there were three or four blisters on his left hand.
"What's this all about?" asked Dr. Ooi. "What's
the matter with all of you?"

Fearful of authority in any form, the fishermen
were at first reluctant to say. Finally one of them
confessed that they had encountered what they
thought was an A-bomb explosion. But when Dr.
Ooi asked them how bright the flash had been, or
whether they had seen the mushroom cloud, their
answers still puzzled him. Since Misaki said that
the light had not been blinding, they must have been
a safe distance away; indeed, if they hadn't been,
some of them should already have died. The men
did not seem seriously ill; their blood counts ran
from 5,000 to 9,000 white cells per cubic centi-
meter—not an alarming decrease. Dr. Ooi wavered,
doubting and believing what their symptoms were.

Five of the patients with bad skin burns he
treated with palliative* ointment, a white paste that
contrasted strangely with their brown-black faces.
Since there was no Geiger counter* in the hospital, and since he could not diagnose radiation sickness with any confidence, Dr. Ooi was not unduly
alarmed over their condition. "Come again tomorrow and let's have an examination with all the doctors," he said, and sent then on their way, greatly
relieved.

---

palliative—temporary remedy.

Geiger counter—device used to test for radioactivity.

But Misaki brooded over the condition of the crew and, after talking with Nishikawa, came back to the hospital later in the afternoon. He asked Dr. Ooi to send two of the men to Tokyo for expert consultation and to write a "letter of favor" for them to someone at the University Hospital. Dr. Ooi, though somewhat miffed at this "rude request," consented. The men he picked were Masuda, because of his heavy burns, and the engineer, Tadashi Yamamoto, because of his low blood count. Dr. Ooi wrote:

The above-mentioned persons, during fishing at Bikini Lagoon area, seemed to have been taken with radiation sickness [*Genbaku-sho*] on March 1. They are supposed to be suffering from atomic cloud of H-bomb. I humbly beg your honorable consultation. . . .

Later Dr. Ooi said that he had used the term "H-bomb" because he had read about it in the newspapers and could not conceive of an A-bomb hurting anyone so far away. He also hoped that such a "big word" might impress the Tokyo doctors who sometimes pay so little attention to the diagnoses of their rural colleagues.

One member of the crew had not been at the hospital. After the *Lucky Dragon* docked, the radioman, Aikichi Kuboyama, feeling shy about his appearance, had gone home by a back road to avoid meeting anyone. And, instead of going in the front door as he usually did, he went around to the back of his house. *"Okaeri-nasai* [welcome home]," his wife called out. "You must be very tired." But his eldest daughter Miyako, when she saw him, said:

"Otoo-chan [papa] looks like a Negro. Look at his face, how black he is!"

Kuboyama told his wife that he did not know exactly what had happened. "On the way home we encountered something—*Gen-Baku* [A-bomb], I think." She looked alarmed and he went on, trying to quiet her, "We saw the blast, but don't worry—we were only covered with ash. I will be well soon." And that same day he went back to the *Lucky Dragon* to repair the radio equipment for the next voyage. It was not until the day after, when one of his crew-mates said he had a low blood count and had been told to rest for two months, that Kuboyama presented himself to the doctors. They gave him some white ointment for his burns and told him that his blood count was 7,200. "It's just an ordinary burn," he told his wife. "There's no need to worry."

Masuda and Yamamoto, the next day, caught the early-morning train to Tokyo. In the washroom of the third-class coach, they looked at their faces in the mirror and were startled to see how dusky and unkempt they looked. They had not shaved and Masuda, in particular, looked quite wild, with his hair seeming to stand out stiffly from his head. He huddled up in his seat in the car and kept silent, glancing sidewise occasionally to see if people were looking at him.

Tokyo University Hospital, when they reached it, looked enormous to the two men. Dimly lit corridors surfaced with a dark linoleum of ancient vintage gave it a depressing atmosphere. Yamamoto, acting as spokesman for the pair, presented his letter to the receptionist and after some misunderstanding with the rather officious clerk, they were directed to Dr. Shimizu's Department of Surgery on the third floor. Yamamoto, who was still clutching a sample of the ash that had fallen on them, showed it to the doctor, who ordered his assistant to bring him a Geiger counter at once. However, it turned out that the instrument was in use and Shimizu turned his full attention to Masuda, paying careful attention to his ears and the thick yellowish discharge that came from them. The man was in worse shape than Yamamoto, and Dr. Shimizu asked him: "Will you, at any rate, enter the hospital for a week?" Sleepy-eyed Masuda nodded that he would and the doctor, after giving orders for him to be registered as an in-patient, left the room. It was after 1:00 P.M. when the two seamen left the hospital. Masuda went with his companion to see if they could find a bite to eat. Afterward Yamamoto went directly to the station, and caught an express back to Yaizu.

Later that same evening, about seven o'clock, Yamamoto went to see the boss, Nishikawa-*san*. He told him that the doctor had said there was nothing to worry about but had asked them to stay in the hospital for a week. "Is it all right?" asked the engineer.

"Sure, sure," replied Nishikawa.

Thus the second day passed after the arrival of the *Lucky Dragon* in port and not a word about it had appeared in the press.

Had there been a daily newspaper in Yaizu, the story of the *Lucky Dragon* might have broken quickly. As it was, the news was delayed—and then splashed over page one of a leading Tokyo paper. This is the story behind the story.

Early in 1954, the *Yomiuri Shimbun,* one of the three largest Japanese newspapers, featured a series of articles on atomic energy. Keiji Kobayashi, a nineteen-year-old student in his second year at

the Shizuoka Prefecture Technical High School, had
been fascinated by them. He felt a kind of personal
interest in the *Yomiuri* newspaper, since a part-time
"leg-man" for it was living as a boarder in his home.
Mitsuyoshi Abe often talked with members of the
Kobayashi family about the value of getting an ex-
clusive story. Scoops are hard to come by in Japan,
where the newspapers employ armies of reporters,
probational reporters, and part-time legmen. The
Asahi Shimbun (Morning Sun) alone employs fifteen
hundred reporters.

Relatives of the family came to visit the Koba-
yashis in the afternoon on March 15, and one of
them mentioned what he had heard from men of the
Lucky Dragon. At dinner that evening young Kobayashi learned about it from his mother. He
remembered saving newspaper clippings about something that had happened on March 1. He dug
through them and found an announcement of the
H-bomb test. Then, thinking of his reporter friend,
he urged his mother to tell Abe-*san* as quickly as
possible. Abe was not in town, however, for he
had gone to the nearby town of Shimada to cover
the killing of a child.

Mrs. Kobayashi placed a long-distance call to
Abe-*san* but could not reach him until it was nearly
dark. As she spilled out the story of the *Lucky Dragon,* Abe interrupted: "What? My father is coming to
Yaizu? I'll be home right away." The quick-witted
reporter knew that unless he gave some plausible
reason for hurrying away the other reporters would
get wise to his story. As it was, they laughed at
Abe. They knew that his father, a Buddhist priest
from a famous spa about fifty miles north of Yaizu,
had sent him money to buy a press camera and
that the money had been squandered on sake.

Shortly after 7:00 P.M. Abe was in Yaizu, and by 7:28 he called the Shizuoka office of the *Yomiuri Shimbun*. Abe-*san* filed a brief story, apparently not fully aware of its news value. He spelled Bikini as Biknik. But the editor on night duty for the *Yomiuri* was Yoshi Tsujiimoto, the very man who edited the atomic energy series which had so interested young Kobayashi. When the news came in from Shizuoka, the editor knew a big story was in the making and he swung into action.

It happened that a reporter by the name of Murao was on duty. He had been on a round-the-world tour and had cooperated on the series of atomic articles. He was hurriedly summoned. Tsujiimoto barked out details. A boat had been near Bikini . . . the crew had been covered with ash . . . the men were burned . . . two crewmen had come to Tokyo that day . . . it was a big story . . . go to Tokyo University at once!

Reporter Murao wasted no time. He picked up a police-beat man and a photographer and they raced to the hospital. When the *Yomiuri* car pulled up in front of the hospital, Murao's heart sank—there in front of the building was a sedan with the flag of the *Asahi Shimbun* attached to the left front fender. An optimist at heart, Murao hoped that the *Asahi* reporter might be there on other business. This he found to be the case. He asked the receptionist: "Did patients with atomic sickness come here today?"

"Yes, they were here today," replied the girl.

Murao was much relieved and thought that his job would be an easy one. But it turned out that these were patients from Hiroshima.* The girl knew

---

Hiroshima—where the first atomic bomb was dropped in World War II.

nothing of any fishermen suffering from atomic sickness. The persistent reporter systematically telephoned each section of the hospital. He got a lucky break when he found an intern who recalled seeing a patient with a "burned-black face" but he could not recall the patient's name or room number. The nurse in charge of night duty denied that any patient from Yaizu had been there that day, but they cajoled her into showing them the list. There was the entry: "Sanjiro Masuda, 29, Yaizu, Shizuoka Prefecture." Then she admitted that Masuda was in the hospital and that Yamamoto, the other patient, had returned to Yaizu. Masuda was sleeping, however, and could not be disturbed. When they pleaded with her she summoned reinforcements—the doctor on duty. He was also adamant. Murao slipped out of the room, determined not to be put off by such resistance. He went from ward to ward, calling softly, "Masuda-*san*," and adding, "man from Yaizu." At last, a patient reacted.

"Yaizu?" he said. "Yes, there's a man in the next room who's suffering from atomic sickness."

His heart pounding like a hunter who has sighted big game, the reporter slipped around the corner and very quietly tiptoed into Room 5. One of the two beds was occupied. The white walls reflected light on the patient, who was curled up on his side. His face was black and his ears were smeared with white ointment. He looked like something from another world, thought Murao, and but for his story he would have fled. Gathering courage, the reporter shook the sleeping man to wake him. Masuda opened his eyes in surprise and sat up. The reporter was astonished at the sight of his swollen hands but he scribbled down the story Masuda told him.

At Yaizu, Abe-*san* had been ordered to interview the crewmen and to get photographs at once. Now he desperately regretted having spent his father's money on sake, for he had no camera. He rushed to the home of a friend, a professional photographer, and woke him up. The two men then hurried to the dock to photograph the fishing boat and the crew.

It was dark on the pier and they found the boat tied up, looking rather forlorn and deserted. The photographer took several flash-bulb shots and Abe-*san* hailed the ship. A lone sailor came on deck and told them that all the others were in town. Some had gone home, some were drinking, and the others —well, they were young and had been at sea for a long time. The reporter knew the drinking spots in town all too well, and he soon found some of the dark-faced crew. They were reluctant to talk, however, for they feared that they would be summoned before authorities. Abe-*san* hunted up Yamamoto and woke him from a sound sleep. He also routed Dr. Ooi from bed and questioned him about the fishermen.

At the night desk of the *Yomiuri* they knew they had a big story—but would it hold? If they broke it in an early edition, say, the one going to cities in western Japan, then the *Asahi* and the *Mainichi,* their two rivals, would pirate the story and run it in tomorrow's Tokyo editions. It was a touch-and-go decision for the *Yomiuri*. The editor decided to hold for the ninth edition and gamble on a real scoop.

Successive editions of the *Yomiuri* rolled off the presses without a mention of the *Lucky Dragon*. Each rival edition of the *Asahi* and the *Mainichi* was rushed to the *Yomiuri* office as fast as it could be snatched up. Each time a new edition hit the desk, the editor and his staff breathed a sigh of relief. Their big story was still safe.

On the morning of Tuesday, March 16, when rival papers could no longer change their morning editions, the *Yomiuri* spread its headline across the front page:

JAPANESE FISHERMEN ENCOUNTERED ATOMIC BOMB TEST AT BIKINI

23 Men Suffering From Atomic Disease
One Diagnosed Serious by Tokyo
University Hospital

H-BOMB?

The story was out at last.

The morning of March 16, some of the seamen from the *Lucky Dragon* knocked off from their chores aboard ship and sauntered down the pier for a walk. They observed a small crowd of people gathered around an electric lamp pole, reading a newspaper tacked up on it. Edging in closer the crewmen from the *Lucky Dragon* were surprised to see that they were in the headlines. They had no idea that what happened to them on March 1 would be of such significance.

If they had any doubts these were soon settled by the swarm of reporters, photographers, television cameramen, and their assistants who descended upon the pier. The decks of the *Lucky Dragon* were soon crowded to overflowing.

The first scientist to arrive at the scene was Professor Takanobu Shiokawa from Shizuoka. He had been at his laboratory that morning in the Chemistry Department of the University of Shizuoka when he received a call from the Prefectural Sanitary Division. He was given a few brief details, supplementing those he had read in the newspaper, and was asked to go to Yaizu and check for radioactivity.

Although the University of Shizuoka is not very pretentious, it does have a well-staffed science department equipped with modern devices for the measurement of radioactivity. Dr. Shiokawa and his assistant hurriedly gathered up some radiation meters and other instruments and then, together with a high prefectural official, they drove over the winding road to Yaizu. After meeting with city officials they drove directly to the hospital and consulted with Dr. Ooi. Two crewmen from the *Lucky Dragon* were already at the hospital and, at Dr. Ooi's request, the scientist inspected the men for traces of radioactivity.

Dr. Shiokawa flipped the "ON" switch of the Geiger counter and waited for a moment for the instrument to warm up. When it was operating properly, Dr. Shiokawa brought it near one of the crewmen. The instrument dial wavered as he brought the counter closer to the sailor, who by this time had taken a close interest in what was going on. Being so slight in stature, the professor stood on tiptoe and brought the counter near the crewman's head. The needle swung over toward the end of the scale! The man was radioactive!

If the men themselves were radioactive, what must the boat be like? Hurrying to the dock, the survey party found the *Lucky Dragon* tied up with fishing boats moored on either side. It was crawling with newsmen, photographing the boat and the crew from every angle. Small clusters of reporters crowded around members of the crew, seeking additional news angles. There was a great hubbub, added to by the din and commotion of carpenters who were making some repairs. When they were still a hundred feet from the boat, Dr. Shiokawa's sensitive Geiger counter started clicking at an accelerated beat. The *Lucky Dragon* was indeed radioactive!

Before going aboard, Dr. Shiokawa carefully checked a little instrument about the size of a fountain pen. It was a pocket meter for adding up the amount of radiation he would receive aboard the boat. Then he climbed aboard, wedging his slender body between the massed humanity on deck. He was astonished at the way the survey instrument needle flipped over to the far side of the scale. Never before had he encountered radioactivity like this.

The technical measurement of radiation involves a considerable knowledge of physics, but it can be understood quite easily on a comparative scale. We can set up a yardstick, putting at the top the amount of radiation (in number of roentgens) required to produce death in an individual, if exposed all over the body. In general, the death range is from 300 to 700 roentgens, although most people would average out in the 400 to 500 bracket. The least amount of radiation which produces an immediately detectable effect in the human body is about 25 roentgens.

It should be emphasized that these figures are for total doses. The readings which Dr. Shiokawa recorded on the decks of the *Lucky Dragon* were of the dose rate—that is, the amount of radiation per hour. As he walked around the crowded decks, he found that the main deck gave a reading of about 25 milliroentgens per hour. Working forward to the prow of the ship, he found it was half that value and, picking his way to the stern, he observed it was several times more radioactive. He ducked into the rear crew compartment, and found that holding the Geiger counter up to the ceiling gave a reading of one-tenth roentgen per hour. Lowering it down to the bunk, he noted that the needle dropped down on the scale and went lower as he shifted the instrument to the lower bunk. It was obvious that the main source of the radioactivity was coming from above, so he climbed up on the roof of the crew space and found that the instrument gave a considerably higher reading. Coils of rope and buoys were stacked on the roof and the scientist soon discovered that these were extremely radioactive. All during their long voyage home the men in the after cabin had been sleeping under an intense source of radiation.

The news that they were radioactive hit the seamen slowly. True, they were horrified when the Geiger counters spluttered and the instruments' needles flipped across the scale. Looking at the scientists and seeing their surprise, the crewmen knew that something most unusual was happening. But it was as though they had been told they had a rare and strange disease; they did not really react until others around them reacted.

An official of the Shizuoka Prefecture told some of the crewmen: "As a result of investigations with the Geiger counter, we find that your hair, nails, and the hull of the ship have a considerable amount of radiation. If left alone as it is, it will surely kill you. We are of the opinion that you should pack your clothes and have them sent to the Prefecture. We are also of the opinion that you should leave the ship." Five of the crewmen agreed to spend the night at the hospital.

Kuboyama, for example, took the news rather stoically. He went back to work on his radio equipment still under the conviction that the ship would put out on a new voyage soon. That night, when he went home and told his wife about the radioactivity, she looked at him blankly as though she had not heard a word he said. Then he mentioned the A-bomb and Hiroshima. She burst into tears and clung to him. The radioman tried to comfort her. "Don't worry, darling, it will take more time to see the results. You go to bed and sleep. We are going to the Yaizu North Hospital tomorrow."

The three children were already asleep. His wife obediently went to bed and Kuboyama stayed up for a while wondering what was in store for him. Later he was to write: "From this day on, unhappiness of our family began."

FURTHER INQUIRY

1. Is radioactive fallout more dangerous than any other form of pollution? Why or why not?
2. Is a family bomb shelter adequate protection from radioactive fallout? Justify your point of view.
3. Why did the reporter feel that he was on the trail of a big story?
4. Why should the people be interested in and worried about what happened to the *Lucky Dragon?*

This selection is from "Silent Spring," a book which became an overnight best seller. One critic says of it that it is a "devastating attack on human carelessness, greed and irresponsibility." For this book the author received eight awards. Albert Schweitzer once said, "Man can hardly even recognize the devils of his own creation." What did he mean? Why might the sprays we use to help trees and plants grow be called "devils of our own creation?"

6

And No Birds Sing

by RACHEL CARSON

F ROM all over the world come echoes of the peril that faces birds in our modern world. The reports differ in detail, but always repeat the theme of death to wildlife in the wake of pesticides.* Such are the stories of hundreds of small birds and

---

pesticides—chemicals used to destroy pests such as flies and mosquitoes.

Reprinted from *Silent Spring* by Rachel Carson by permission of the publisher, Houghton Mifflin Company.

Within five years after DDT was developed, crop losses were cut by 90 percent. Usually planes spray DDT over wide areas. (Bell Aircraft)

partridges dying in France after vine stumps were treated with an arsenic-containing herbicide, or of partridge shoots in Belgium, once famous for the numbers of their birds, denuded of partridges after the spraying of nearby farmlands.

In England the major problem seems to be a specialized one, linked with the growing practice of treating seed with insecticides* before sowing. Seed treatment is not a wholly new thing, but in earlier years the chemicals principally used were fungicides. No effects on birds seem to have been noticed. Then about 1956 there was a change to dual-purpose treatment; in addition to a fungicide, dieldrin, aldrin, or heptachlor* was added to combat soil insects. Thereupon the situation changed for the worse.

In the spring of 1960 a deluge of reports of dead birds reached British wildlife authorities, including the British Trust for Ornithology*, the Royal Society for the Protection of Birds, and the Game Birds Association. "The place is like a battlefield," a landowner in Norfolk wrote. "My keeper has found innumerable corpses, including masses of small birds —chaffinches, greenfinches, linnets, hedge sparrows, also house sparrows . . . the destruction of wild life is quite pitiful." A gamekeeper wrote: "My partridges have been wiped out with the dressed corn, also some pheasants and all other birds, hundreds of birds have been killed. . . . As a lifelong gamekeeper it has been a distressing experience for

---

insecticides—chemicals used to kill insects.

dieldrin, aldrin, heptachlor—chemicals used to kill soil insects.

ornithology—study of birds.

me. It is bad to see pairs of partridges that have
died together."

In a joint report, the British Trust for Ornithology
and the Royal Society for the Protection of Birds
described some 67 kills of birds—a far from com-
plete listing of the destruction that took place in the
spring of 1960. Of these 67, 59 were caused by seed
dressings, 8 by toxic sprays.

A new wave of poisoning set in the following
year. The death of 600 birds on a single estate in
Norfolk was reported to the House of Lords, and
100 pheasants died on a farm in North Essex.
It soon became evident that more counties were
involved than in 1960 (34 compared with 23). Lin-
colnshire, heavily agricultural, seemed to have suffered most, with reports of 10,000 birds dead. But
destruction involved all of agricultural England, from
Angus in the north to Cornwall in the south, from
Anglesey in the west to Norfolk in the east.

In the spring of 1961 concern reached such a
peak that a special committee of the House of Commons made an investigation of the matter, taking
testimony from farmers, landowners, and represen-
tatives of the Ministry of Agriculture and of various
governmental and nongovernmental agencies concerned with wildlife.

"Pigeons are suddenly dropping out of the sky
dead," said one witness. "You can drive a hundred
or two hundred miles outside London and not see a
single kestrel," reported another. "There has been
no parallel in the present century, or at any time
so far as I am aware . . . [this is] the biggest risk to
wildlife and game that ever occurred in the country," officials of the Nature Conservancy testified.

Facilities for chemical analysis of the victims
were most inadequate to the task, with only two

chemists in the country able to make the tests (one the government chemist, the other in the employ of the Royal Society for the Protection of Birds). Witnesses described huge bonfires on which the bodies of the birds were burned. But efforts were made to have carcasses collected for examination, and of the birds analyzed, all but one contained pesticide residues. The single exception was a snipe, which is not a seed-eating bird.

Along with the birds, foxes may also have been affected, probably indirectly by eating poisoned mice or birds. England, plagued by rabbits, sorely needs the fox as predator. But between November 1959 and April 1960 at least 1300 foxes died. Deaths were heaviest in the same counties from which sparrow hawks, kestrels, and other birds of prey had virtually disappeared, suggesting that the poison was spreading through the food chain, reaching out from the seed eaters to the furred and feathered carnivores. The actions of the moribund* foxes were those of animals poisoned by chlorinated hydrocarbon insecticides. They were seen wandering in circles, dazed and half blind, before dying in convulsions.

The hearings convinced the committee that the threat to wildlife was "most alarming"; it accordingly recommended to the House of Commons that "the Minister of Agriculture and the Secretary of State for Scotland should secure the immediate prohibition for the use as seed of dressings of compounds containing dieldrin, aldrin, or heptachlor, or chemicals of comparable toxicity." The committee also recommended more adequate controls to ensure that

---

predator—animal that preys on other animals.

moribund—in a dying state.

chemicals were adequately tested under field as well as laboratory conditions before being put on the market. This, it is worth emphasizing, is one of the great blank spots in pesticide research everywhere. Manufacturers' tests on the common laboratory animals—rats, dogs, guinea pigs—include no wild species, no birds as a rule, no fishes, and are conducted under controlled and artificial conditions. Their application to wildlife in the field is anything but precise.

England is by no means alone in its problem of protecting birds from treated seeds. Here in the United States the problem has been most troublesome in the rice-growing areas of California and the South. For a number of years California rice growers have been treating seed with DDT as protection against tadpole shrimp and scavenger beetles which sometimes damage seedling rice. California sportsmen have enjoyed excellent hunting because of the concentration of waterfowl and pheasants in the rice fields. But for the past decade persistent reports of bird losses, especially among pheasants, ducks, and blackbirds, have come from the rice-growing counties. "Pheasant sickness" became a well-known phenomenon: birds "seek water, become paralyzed, and are found on the ditch banks and rice checks quivering," according to one observer. The "sickness" comes in the spring, at the time the rice fields are seeded. The concentration of DDT used is many times the amount that will kill an adult pheasant.

The passage of a few years and the development of even more poisonous insecticides served to increase the hazard from treated seed. Aldrin, which is 100 times as toxic as DDT to pheasants, is now widely used as a seed coating. In the rice fields of eastern Texas, this practice has seriously reduced

Baby eagle and brother that never hatched. Accumulated DDT in the body of the mother may have caused thin-shelled egg—a poor incubator for the unborn. (Michigan Department of Natural Resources)

the populations of the fulvous tree duck, a tawny-colored gooselike duck of the Gulf Coast. Indeed, there is some reason to think that the rice growers, having found a way to reduce the populations of blackbirds, are using the insecticide for a dual purpose, with disastrous effects on several bird species of the rice fields.

As the habit of killing grows—the resort to "eradicating" any creature that may annoy or inconvenience us—birds are more and more finding themselves a direct target of poisons rather than an incidental one. There is a growing trend toward aerial applications of such deadly poisons as parathion to "control" concentrations of birds distasteful to farmers. The Fish and Wildlife Service has found it necessary to express serious concern over this trend, pointing out that "parathion-treated areas constitute a potential hazard to humans, domestic animals, and wildlife." In southern Indiana, for example, a group of farmers went together in the summer of 1959 to engage a spray plane to treat an area of river bottomland with parathion. The area was a favored roosting site for thousands of blackbirds that were feeding in nearby cornfields. The problem could have been solved easily by a slight change in agricultural practice—a shift to a variety of corn with deep-set ears not accessible to the birds—but the farmers had been persuaded of the merits of killing by poison, and so they sent in the planes on their mission of death.

The results probably gratified the farmers, for the casualty list included some 65,000 red-winged blackbirds and starlings. What other wildlife deaths may have gone unnoticed and unrecorded is not known. Parathion is not a specific for blackbirds: it is a universal killer. But such rabbits or raccoons or opossums as may have roamed those bottomlands and perhaps never visited the farmers' cornfields were doomed by a judge and jury who neither knew of their existence nor cared.

And what of human beings? In California orchards sprayed with this same parathion, workers handling foliage that had been treated a month earlier collapsed and went into shock, and escaped death only through skilled medical attention. Does Indiana still raise any boys who roam through woods and fields and might even explore the margins of a river? If so, who guarded the poisoned area to keep out any who might wander in, in misguided search for unspoiled nature? Who kept vigilant watch to tell the innocent stroller that the fields he was about to enter were deadly—all their vegetation coated with a lethal film? Yet at so fearful a risk the farmers, with none to hinder them, waged their needless war on blackbirds.

In each of these situations, one turns away to ponder the question: Who has made the decision that sets in motion these chains of poisoning, this ever-widening wave of death that spreads out, like ripples when a pebble is dropped into a still pond? Who has placed in one pan of the scales the leaves that might have been eaten by the beetles and in the other the pitiful heaps of many-hued feathers, the lifeless remains of the birds that fell before the unselective bludgeon of insecticidal poisons? Who has decided—who has the RIGHT to decide—for the countless legions of people who were not consulted that the supreme value is a world without insects, even though it be also a sterile world ungraced by the curving wing of a bird in flight? The decision is that of the authoritarian temporarily entrusted with power; he has made it during a moment of inattention by millions to whom beauty and the ordered world of nature still have a meaning that is deep and imperative.

FURTHER INQUIRY

1. Is the use of chemical sprays ever justified? When? Defend your point of view.
2. How may destroying one form of life (insect) to protect another form of life (plant) destroy the balance (ecology) that exists among living things?

There is little doubt that there is a close relationship between air pollution and disease as this article amply demonstrates. There is an equally close relationship between smoking and disease as well. Although air pollution may be difficult to control, each person can control the smoking habit.

7

Air Pollution and Disease

by U.S. DEPARTMENT OF HEALTH, EDUCATION, AND WELFARE

UNLESS gas masks are to become a habitual part of our dress, we must breathe the air as it comes to us, polluted or not. For most of us, more often than not the air is polluted with a host of gases and particles which we pump into our lungs and swallow into our stomachs. Some pollutants sting our eyes and throats, and others affront

U.S. Department of Health, Education, and Welfare. *The Effects of Air Pollution.* Public Health Service Publication No. 1556, U.S. Government Printing Office, 1967, Washington, D.C.

Patients with lung problems are given breathing tests in this "body box" at St. Vincent's Hospital and Medical Center in New York. The equipment is also used in research studies to trace the effects of pollutants such as sulfur dioxide when inhaled. (R. J. Henning, St. Vincent's Hospital)

our noses. Still others find their way into our bloodstream, where they travel up and down the body,
working their toxic ways as they go.

It is in our respiratory system, and particularly in
our lungs, that we are most vulnerable to air pollution. Life depends on the steady supply of oxygen
from the lungs to the blood, and the steady removal
of carbon dioxide from the blood by the lungs. These
gases are transferred through hundreds of tiny balloons whose skins are one ten-thousandth of an inch
thick. This delicate tissue, if spread flat, would cover
a tennis court, and when we are born we have many
more balloons than we need for breathing. But one
of the cumulative effects of air pollution (along
with smoking and disease) is the progressive destruction of these balloons, and as we grow older,
we lose some of our lung reserve. Unfortunately
for many of us, we are not aware of the loss until
much of our reserve is gone. And the damage is
irreparable. . . .

The air pollution disasters are alarming enough,
but of even greater concern to those of us who
live in polluted air, and that includes most of us, are
the long term effects of the air pollution that begins
to assail us from the day of our birth. With every
breath we take, an increasing percentage of
us come a little closer to a diagnosable diseased
condition. These ills are mostly diseases of the bronchial tree—from the common cold to lung cancer.
But air pollution also irritates the eyes, and some
pollutants in the air, like lead, may build up in the
body until they reach harmful levels. Others, like
carbon monoxide, are not cumulative in their effects, but in high enough concentrations can cause
temporary disability, and even death.

Emphysema is a progressive breakdown of air

sacs in the lungs usually brought on by chronic infection or irritation of the bronchial tubes, and which progressively diminishes the ability of the lungs to transfer oxygen to the bloodstream and carbon dioxide from it.

Today in this country, emphysema is the fastest growing cause of death. In the 10 year period between 1950 and 1959 deaths among males from emphysema rose from 1.5 per hundred thousand to 8 per hundred thousand. In 1962 more than 12,000 persons died of emphysema in the United States and each month 1,000 more workers are forced prematurely to retire onto Social Security rolls because of the disease.

Studies have demonstrated that emphysema patients improve when they are protected from air pollution. In one study, emphysema patients exposed to photochemical smog expressed subjective relief and showed objective improvement when the air was filtered. The fact that the incidence of emphysema is greater in our cities than in our rural areas points to air pollution as a contributing factor, as does the fact that deaths from emphysema are twice as high in the city as in the country.

The criteria for diagnosing *chronic bronchitis* have yet to be standardized in this country. In Great Britain, where the criteria are defined as chronic productive cough, nearly 10 percent of all deaths and more than 10 percent of all industrial absences because of illness are attributed to this disease. Using the British criteria, one investigation in this country found chronic bronchitis in 21 percent of men 40 to 59 years old. Other studies indicate that 13 to 20 percent of adult males in this country have the disease.

In Great Britain, where more attention has been

given to the disease and where more data are available, cigarette smoking and air pollution are accepted as distinct causes of chronic bronchitis. The mortality rate from the disease in Great Britain has been found to vary directly with such air pollution measures as population density, amount of fuel burned, sulfur dioxide levels, settled dust, airborne dust, and decreased visibility. Known sufferers of the disease who were systematically observed showed a worsening of their symptoms on days of higher air pollution.

Chronic constrictive ventilatory disease is a long continued constriction of the air passages that requires extra effort in breathing. Healthy persons may not notice the extra effort, but for those whose lungs or hearts are already functioning marginally, such effort may be unbearable.

Laboratory experimental work with both animals and humans has shown that such irritant pollutants as sulfur oxides, at levels routinely found in our city air, can produce airway constriction, and thus may lead to the chronic disease. And the disease is not confined to the city. In a study of two Pennsylvania towns, each with a population of slightly less than 1,000, and whose environments differed principally in the levels of air pollution, airway resistance was higher in the people living in the town with higher levels of air pollution.

Bronchial asthma is a condition often aggravated by air pollution. However, since the list of stimuli capable of triggering asthmatic attacks is long, it is difficult to define precisely the role of air pollutants. It has long been known that occupational exposure to certain dusts and vapors, including many that are sometimes found in substantial quantities in the air over our cities, can bring about asthmatic attacks. The previously mentioned Donora [Pennsylvania] tragedy provided a striking example of the role of air pollution in aggravating asthma attacks and even in bringing death to some asthmatics.

A special form of asthma appeared in 1946 among American troops and their dependents living in Yokohama, Japan. The disease later appeared among our troops in Tokyo, and it was given the name *Tokyo-Yokohama asthma,* or *T-Y asthma.* The disease did not yield to the usual asthma specifics; however, patients usually recovered if they were promptly removed from the area upon becoming afflicted. Studies showed that the incidence of the disease and the severity of attacks correlated best with levels of air pollution, which had its origins in the heavily industrialized Kanto Plain, extending between Yokohama and Tokyo.

In New Orleans, epidemic outbreaks of asthma attacks have been associated with certain wind conditions. When the attacks first occurred, they were associated with particulate matter discharged into the air when certain abandoned city dumps spontaneously caught fire underground. Further investigation, however, indicated that other sources of air pollution contributed to the outbreaks.

Many investigations have connected air pollution with the incidence of the *common cold.* A study in a Maryland city of two groups of people who differed, for the most part, only in the amounts of particulate matter they were exposed to, found that the group living in the more polluted section of town had more colds. In a large-scale study of absenteeism in industrial plants widely scattered throughout the United States it was found that levels of air pollution correlate with increased frequency of acute infections of the upper respiratory tract. Investigations in Great

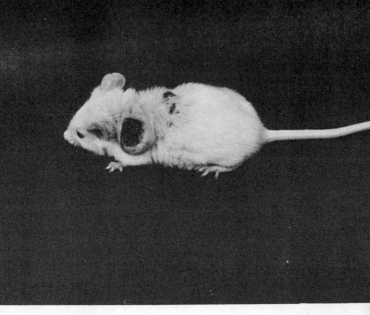

Skin cancer on mouse developed after its skin was painted with pollutants from urban air. (U.S. Public Health Service)

Britain, Japan, and the Soviet Union have confirmed the American findings.

Experiments in the laboratory have repeatedly shown that animals forced to inhale some of the irritating gases commonly found in community atmospheres are more vulnerable to *pneumonia* organisms than animals not exposed to the gases.

Deaths from *lung cancer* have been increasing rapidly in recent years, and while many factors are probably involved, the striking difference between the urban and rural mortality rate for lung cancer points to one of them—air pollution. The rate in our large metropolitan areas is twice the rural rate, even after full allowance is made for differences in smoking habits. The death rate from lung cancer is apparently directly proportional to city size, and the same can be said, in general, for levels of air pollution.

Four independent studies have shown that long-time residence in countries with different degrees of air pollution was associated with different incidences of lung cancer. In one study, for example, of a Norwegian group that emigrated to America the incidence of lung cancer was halfway between the incidence in Norwegians who stayed at home and the incidence in native Americans. In Norway, where there is much less air pollution, the lung cancer rate is half that of the United States.

Laboratory investigations have provided further clues. In one study, mice that had been sensitized with influenza virus and then exposed to ozonized gasoline (simulated photochemical smog) developed bronchogenic cancer of the type humans develop. In another study, hamsters exposed repeatedly to intratracheal administrations of a particulate form of hydrocarbon that is found much more frequently in city air than in rural air, all developed bronchogenic cancer.

FURTHER INQUIRY

1. Which diseases may be related to air pollution?
2. How did Tokyo asthma get its name?
3. What significance, if any, may be attached to the fact that immigrants from Norway had a higher rate of lung cancer than Norwegians who remained in their own country?
4. Cigarette packages now contain the message, "Smoking may be hazardous to health." What hazards are they referring to?

Senator Robert F. Kennedy was assassinated in June, 1968. Before he died he had commented on many aspects of American society. Not the least of these, was the need to do something about air pollution. In the speech that follows he explained what he thought might have been done. The speech was given on February 1, 1968 at the New York-New Jersey Air Abatement Conference.

8

Air Pollution and the Death of Our Cities

by ROBERT F. KENNEDY

SINCE we last met, we have learned from Dr. Leonard Greenburg, of the Albert Einstein College of Medicine, that the blackened air of our cities carries within it death. During that smog emergency of 1966, the poison in our air killed 186 persons. And this was only the immediate effect; many

Reprinted with permission from *Social Action,* Vol. XXXIV, No. 9, May, 1968. Copyright © 1968 by the Council for Christian Social Action of the United Church of Christ.

more of our citizens will die from the effects of this smog for years to come.

The conclusion is clear: we no longer debate what we have to do. The question we face now is what to do about it. For air pollution now is more than an unpleasant sensation, more than the filth which defines our modern cities. Pollution will—as a certainty—make the city uninhabitable within our lifetimes unless it is reversed. Pollution will kill hundreds—perhaps thousands—of us. if we do not wage a vigorous fight to eliminate it. When we begin talk-

This view of Manhattan from Queens showing the Con Edison smoke stacks was taken during an air pollution air survey. Even on a good day New York loses almost 25% of its light to smoke and smog. (Wide World)

ing of "smog shelters" to protect our older, less healthy individuals, when we begin to consider covering our cities to save us from our own atmosphere, we can understand that this subject—technical as it is—has a crucial immediate, human concern. Either we will eliminate pollution from our cities, or pollution will eliminate the cities. The choice is that clear; so is the need to act.

We have already taken an important first step. We have made it clear—on all levels of government—that as a matter of clear public policy, the pollution of our atmosphere will no longer be tolerated. Ever since 1955, when Congress found the need "to protect the nation's air resources . . . to promote the public health and welfare . . ." governments have been attempting to draft effective legislation against pollution.

Words are not actions; and declarations do not clean our atmosphere. But government, after all, is the expression of public concern. A firm refusal to tolerate pollution is an important victory—*if* that refusal is supported by forceful government action.

Yet, disturbingly, this firm action is missing. For despite all the promises and proclamations, government itself is a principal polluter of our air. The very force which should be moving vigorously to make clean air a reality in the New York metropolitan area is itself a chief cause of our dilemma.

Federal Offenders

In 1965, for example, the Air Pollution Abatement Council surveyed the 17-county area of its jurisdiction to discover who were "federal offenders" —those emitting 100 tons or more of sulfur oxide pollutants. In that year, the last for which official figures are available, the Council found 373 "federal offenders." Almost half of them were *publicly owned enterprises:* hospitals, public housing units, public utilities. And there is every indication that conditions have worsened since then. Fully 105 of the 373 offenders were public housing units; built and operated by local governments with federal assistance. And, while their contribution was relatively small—22,000 tons out of 871,000—this was not true of other public facilities.

The 11 Public Service Corporations which serve New Jersey were the second worst "federal offender" —reponsible for the emission of more than 266,000 tons of sulfur oxide pollutants in 1965. And here in New York, Consolidated Edison—the publicly regulated utility supplying electric power for New York City—was found to be the single worst federal offender, contributing more than 367,000 tons into our atmosphere.

Nor is the picture substantially different when we talk of particulate emission. Power plants—almost all of them government operated or regulated—contributed 17.3 percent of all particulate emissions in 1966, according to the joint study made for this conference. Municipal incineration added another 8.7 percent; public housing and government buildings played a substantial part in adding another 5-10 percent to our atmosphere. And New York City's buses—those delightful smoke machines which New York pedestrians greet with such joy—gave us a significant part of the 35,000 tons emitted by motor vehicles.

These violations of federal standards and common sense are diverse; many of them can be explained by the neglect and indifference of the past, which permitted private and public sector alike to build without regard to pollution consequences. Further, government on all levels has begun to correct a major share of these deficiencies.

But these failures—and the meaning they have—cannot be understood in a vacuum. They exist today when air pollution becomes each day a more imminent threat to our health and our lives. They exist at a time when we have made it a matter of public policy to move and move now against the poisoning of our air. They exist when we are moving to confront those who will not take rapid and effective steps to end pollution.

Thus, each day that we permit our public facilities to remain as major air polluters, each day that major utilities foul the atmosphere with sulfur oxides and particulates—each of these days is another day in which government says to industry and citizen: "We don't really mean it. We don't really think pollution is all that bad; there is no crisis—pollution as usual."

Intolerance Recommended

In my judgment, the time is too late for continued toleration of pollution; the danger is too great to permit any polluter to change at his convenience. But this is true especially of the public sector, which is supposed to chart public policy. How can the city demand of private enterprise rapid action—if it permits its own facilities to continue to violate federal standards? How can the federal government declare the necessity of clean air if it finances and operates buildings which themselves pollute?

The short answer is, it cannot. We in public life, and those private citizens who have contributed so much to public concern about pollution, can no lon-

ger meet a real, present crisis with indifference.
The public sector must take immediate, effective
steps to end its own contribution to pollution.

There are, I think, five essential elements of an
effective program:

First, the federal government must take a far
more vigorous role in supporting local efforts to control pollution.

As a first step, no public buildings should be au-
thorized or approved unless they meet stringent pollution control standards.

Many federal buildings, despite the regulations
imposed by city and state, may well be in the plan-
ning stage now with little or no attention having
been focused on the pollution consequences. To
avoid this, I would urge agencies at all levels to review their construction plans to insure that effective
pollution controls have been established. The General Services Agency plans substantial construction
for fiscal 1969 in the New York Metropolitan area;
and hundreds more units of publicly-supported housing are being erected. It is essential that these buildings include rigid limits on pollution; just as it is
essential for government agencies in the future to be
as concerned over pollution as they now are about
any other element of safety.

Similarly, the federal government must cooperate
in converting its own facilities to meet pollution
problems. For example, despite repeated offers from
a local gas distributor, the Federal Office Building
in Brooklyn has still not converted to gas and dis-
tillate fuels—and the Corps of Engineers have still
not instituted an acceptable method of disposing of
burnable wastes collected from the harbor.

Further, we must encourage the acceleration of
conversion by utilities to low-sulfur fuel consump-

tion. Consolidated Edison has already announced that they will move up the 1971 deadline on conversion to 1 percent fuel. This is gratifying; but it can only be accomplished with help from all parts of the government. For example, Con Ed and other utilities have experienced difficulty in finding an adequate supply of low-sulfur fuel—principally number 2 fuel—because of continuing domestic shortages. Here is an area where federal help is needed—in the form of liberalized imports—to provide low-sulfur fuel at reasonable prices.

I have already been in touch with Interior Secretary Udall, urging that the Department of the Interior begin to reëvaluate our present rigid oil-import limits. In my judgment, the simple heating of homes requires liberalization. But if we add to home heating the immense need of utilities, a greatly increased supply of number 2 fuel becomes a national necessity. And I would hope the Interior Department begins to move quickly in this direction.

The Federal Power Commission has already begun its cooperation by granting an additional 20 billion cubic feet of gas to Con Ed; I hope the Department of the Interior will assist this vital work.

Second, we should begin—immediately—to equip our existing government buildings with stack emission control devices. These devices are capable of capturing up to 99 percent of emissions, thus dramatically reducing particulates in our atmosphere. Rapid adoption of these devices is an essential part of any coordinated public attack on pollution.

Third, state and local governments must begin now to enforce already existing regulations. Surveys, air quality measurements, studies—these are valuable tools; but these tools must be used to enforce effective restrictions. Here in New York City, for example, effective enforcement of Local Law 14 and the air pollution control code would reduce particulate emissions by 47 percent. And, as your pre-conference report notes, if this metropolitan region enforced its own pollution laws, we could cut back by 37 percent from the dangerous 1966 particulate emission levels.

Fourth, municipal transportation ought to move immediately to a serious consideration of electrically-powered buses. Electrically-run motor vehicles may well be impractical for long-range, high-speed travel. But there is no reason why buses, which travel relatively short distances each day, cannot be developed with electric motors. This development would radically change one of the most annoying of all pollution irritants suffered by New York residents.

Fifth, and most broadly, we might well begin to consider whether the public sector can afford to ignore private pollution in its own procurement policies. Across a wide range of behavior, this government enforces fundamental public decisions. Government contractors, for example, must pay minimum —and in some cases the prevailing—wages, to prevent government-subsidized sweatshops. Contracts will not—at least, officially—be let to firms which practice racial discrimination; thus minimizing government-subsidized prejudice. Food and drugs will not be dispensed by public agencies if they do not meet strict criteria; thus fighting government-subsidized disease. And only recently, the General Services Administration began requiring safety standards for autos bought by the government; thus ending government-subsidized injury.

In my judgment, the time may have come to make a similar decision regarding government-subsidized pollution. Most government agencies purchase all

MAJOR GROWTH TRENDS AFFECTING AIR POLLUTION

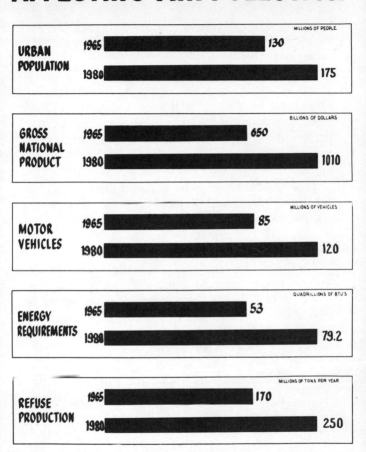

Major growth trends affecting air pollution (National Center for Air Pollution Control)

goods from manufacturers on a bidding basis; these manufacturers submit cost and time estimates, as well as data on quality. We may well have to begin requiring that government contractors provide assurance of compliance with already-existing air pollution standards.

At present, each manufacturer, each industry points across a river, or across a county line, to excuse his own neglect. But by imposing government standards on all manufacturers, through the bidding device, we would insure a rapid attempt to bring industry into compliance with established standards.

This step would not be accomplished overnight. We should recognize that industry will need assistance—and perhaps a form of federal subsidy, through tax deductions or credits—to assume the cost of converting to low-pollution standards.

But it is a step which must be taken. The citizenry will no longer tolerate continued indifference—by either public or private sector—to the hazards poured into the atmosphere each day. If we in public life really mean what we say—if the menace of air pollution is more than rhetoric—we should demonstrate our sincerity by moving *now* to wipe it out. If we buy products from those who pollute the air, or if government itself helps make this region uninhabitable in 2 years, we will have proved only our capacity for hypocrisy. And we will have helped to destroy the greatest metropolitan area in the world.

It was Edmund Burke who told an earlier generation that ". . . they should not think it amongst their rights to . . . commit waste on the inheritance, by destroying at their pleasure the whole original fabric of their society; hazarding to leave to those who come after them a ruin instead of a habitation."

This generation has tasted the bitter fruit of the waste we have committed on our priceless inheritance of natural wonder. Now we are beginning to understand that this waste will indeed breed a ruin—in the form of poisonous air, crippling and killing instead of sustaining us. We have declared again and again that this is not to be our fate. Now declaration is not enough; action is imperative. And it is we—in public life—who will bear the heaviest responsibility if our action is not fully responsive to the menace in our air.

FURTHER INQUIRY

1. Why did Senator Kennedy say that New Yorkers need no research studies to tell them what air pollution means?
2. Do you agree or disagree with Senator Kennedy when he said, "Either we will eliminate pollution from our cities, or pollution will eliminate the cities?"
3. Why did Senator Kennedy say that government itself is a principal polluter of our air? What examples of this can he give? To what extent was the Senator right?
4. How can government force private industry to reduce pollution?

What happened on Doremus Avenue in Newark, New Jersey may be taken as a case study of what can be done about air pollution. What follows is a description of the problems one man faced as he tried to make the law effective.

9

One Man Made a Difference

from AIRSAN

DOREMUS Avenue, Newark. It's a street flanked by industry and troubled by air pollution. A challenge to the operatives engaged in control.

A young man . . . helped to arrest the contamination. It's not all arrested yet, but this man, part of a dedicated group, has placed a lid at least partially over the pollution. His name is Allan Edwards.

From *AirSan*, May-June, 1966. State of New Jersey, Department of Health, Division of Clean Air and Water, Trenton, New Jersey. Reprinted with permission.

Allan, under the supervision of John Tozzi, Supervisor of the Metropolitan Field Office, Air Sanitation Program, New Jersey State Department of Health, has achieved a significant start on the abatement* of air pollution in the Doremus Avenue section of Newark. The section, triangular, two and one-half square miles in area, is shaped like New Hampshire in reverse. . . .

Look east as you're headed north on the Turnpike, after you've passed well beyond Exit 14. No, you can't see Doremus Avenue itself, but you can make out the long lines of bizarre industrial structures that parallel the street as it stretches northeastward toward the gnarled ramps of the Pulaski Skyway.

Fractionating towers.* Crazy mazes of pipes. Tank farms. Chemical plants. Metallurgical operations. Slaughter houses. Fat-rendering plants. Small manufacturing establishments and big ones. Railroad tank cars. And trucks . . . roaring and laborious.

Overhead, one of the air traffic approaches to Newark Airport. About 700 planes to, in and out of the airport daily.

The Turnpike: over 60,000 cars a day pass in both directions between Exits 14 and 15.

The Viaduct, a short distance west of the Turnpike; traffic count . . . 71,970 daily.

Along the river and the shore of Newark Bay, port facilities for small tankers and barges.

Astride the Turnpike, junkyards and landfills.

This is Doremus Avenue, a propagator of products vital to the nation. A street with myriad sources

---

abatement—lessening.

fractionating towers—where a substance such as oil is broken down into different products.

of air pollution. Once, decades ago, this section was a meadow. Birds nested in the marshes. Then it became a garbage disposal area. The land was filled in. Now, it is an industrial complex. Natives call it the "Down Neck" section. From its caldron pours basic stuffs from which America manufactures its products—resins for plastics, dyes for fabrics, pigments for inks, sulfuric acid for many uses, alum and chlorine for water purifiers, synthetic ethyl alcohol for perfumes, cresylic acid for disinfectants and plastics, tallow for soaps, tin for tin cans, methyl chloride for refrigerants . . . the inventory is much longer.

The atmospheric effluent* from all these industrial processes is rich indeed. It is wafted eastward across

atmospheric effluent—outflow of smoke and odors.

Astride the turnpike, ugly junkyards and dumps are an eyesore. (Bruce Davidson, Magnum)

the Passaic River . . . westward to parts of Newark, north-south along the Turnpike, and of course, up and down Doremus Avenue itself. More than one manufacturer on the street has complained about the stench his neighbors are putting out.

Air Sanitation's Metropolitan Field Office started functioning in Newark last October [1965]. It became quickly apparent that air pollution from the Doremus Avenue plants was endangering health and welfare. Complaints from all around its perimeter came into Tozzi's office. Men he sent out to check on complaints identified odors such as mercaptan,* fish oil, and sulfur compounds. Allan Edwards was one of the men. . . .

But Tozzi and his superiors in Trenton realized

mercaptan—chemical with very bad odor.

that this would not do the trick. What was needed was a house-to-house cleansing of the entire Doremus Avenue area. They proposed broadening the scope of the activity to project size and doing a saturation type of enforcement program. . . .

In plant after plant, Allan sat down with plant manager or plant superintendent. He made it clear that there is a serious air pollution situation. He recited the applicable provisions of the New Jersey Air Pollution Control Code and put copies of the code into their hands. He gathered information on products produced, raw materials used, manufacturing processes and air pollution control measures. Some of the plants were contributing little or no pollution to the atmosphere. He set up files on them nonetheless. The polluters, however, he visited again and again. He recommended consultation with engineering consultants on control devices. . . . He examined with them possible changes in their processes of manufacture. . . . He asked them for periodic reports on progress.

This way of achieving air pollution control has been going on for years in New Jersey. . . . It gets results; it accomplishes significant abatement; and it does so without fanfare, without formal hearings, court actions, fines, plant closures and disruption of the economy. Not that such strong measures could not ultimately result—they could, if firms fail to show satisfactory progress.

FURTHER INQUIRY

1. Why should air pollution in New Jersey concern New York as well?
2. To what extent can the methods used on Doremus Avenue be used elsewhere?

While the misuse of atomic energy can bring the bomb and with it radioactive fallout, the peaceful use of atomic energy can help end air pollution. In this selection scientists, looking into the future, see a possible end to air pollution. Why are scientists hopeful that nuclear power will help solve the problem of air pollution?

10

Smog Worry Brings a Rush to Nuclear Power

from THE NATIONAL OBSERVER

"**I**T is conceivable that the future will see vast, automated industrial complexes built around large nuclear power plants. . . . Such a complex would be quiet, clean, and compact. . . . Few if any chimneys would rise from this complex, in which all potential pollutants would be carefully controlled."

From *The National Observer,* Feb. 13, 1967. Reprinted with permission.

By 1971, Con Edison will have a third nuclear electric generating unit at Indian Point, Buchanan, New York. (Con Edison)

This long look toward a clearer day for the nation's smog-clogged cities comes from Dr. Glenn T. Seaborg, chairman of the Atomic Energy Commission (AEC). Recently, Dr. John Ray Dunning, Dean of Columbia University's School of Engineering and Applied Science . . . looked to the more immediate future. City councils in smog-troubled cities, he predicted, soon will be banning the use of fossil fuels* (coal, oil, gas) by electrical generating plants. The power companies will have to use nuclear energy instead.

Subsequent developments suggest that both sci-

---

fossil fuels—given this name because coal, oil, and gas were formed millions of years ago when the earth was relatively young.

entists' predictions may come true sooner than either had anticipated. Fossil fuels have just been banned in a major U.S. metropolis. And a trend toward the use of nuclear energy to generate electricity has become a rush. . . .

At a Surprising Rate

Indeed, the growth of nuclear-fueled power plants is far faster than anyone anticipated when the nation began searching for peaceful uses for nuclear energy. . . .

Consider:

The major builders of electrical generating systems are backlogged with orders for nuclear-fueled systems. . . .

There are 14 nuclear power plants in operation in the United States. . . .

Major nuclear plants are now being built without federal subsidy because power companies have concluded that in many areas, they will be more economical than fossil-fueled plants.

The ballooning interest in nuclear power plants has set off a new mining rush for uranium to fuel the plants.

Scientists working to develop a second generation of . . . nuclear reactors, which will create their own fuel supply at the same time they are driving electrical generators, are optimistic that they will succeed within a few years.

The big switch to nuclear power is having major economic side effects, principally to coal and to oil and gas producers. But in one sense, the individual consumer of electricity sees no change. The electricity flowing through his meter is the same whether generated by nuclear, fossil, or water energy. . . .

Cleaner Air Expected

In more significant areas, though, the consumer may experience major changes. His electric bill, for example, likely will decrease if the breeder of nuclear reactors is perfected. And . . . the air he breathes will be cleaner. . . .

FURTHER INQUIRY

1. What advantages does nuclear power have over fossil fuels such as coal, oil, or gas?
2. How are the coal, oil, and gas industries likely to be affected by the growth of nuclear power?

At one time America was a land of unpolluted forests, streams, rivers, and air. Today there are few, if any, places left that have not been poisoned. How we have abused our most beautiful and vital resources is the substance of this article. Why does the author say that what we have done to our waters is a national disgrace?

11

Our Dying Waters

by JOHN BIRD

THIS is the story of a national disgrace.

We Americans were privileged to start our national life on a virtually unused, unspoiled continent. The country which became the United States was vast and beautiful, a landscape of mountains, valleys and plains, all drained by one of the world's most generous systems of waters: crystal-clear mountain brooks, meandering lowland creeks, great rolling rivers, massive fresh-water lakes and salty bays and estuaries.* Here was a primary source of life, wealth, and enjoyment beyond measure, it seemed to our forefathers—enough good water to meet the nation's needs for all time to come. Yet, within a few generations we have fouled and degraded our beautiful waters. With destructive ignorance and vandalistic abandon we have clogged the capillaries and arteries of our land with filth. Perhaps we were lulled in the early days by the reassuring platitude

---

estuaries—part of river's mouth where it reaches the sea.

Here are a few of several hundred bass and big goldfish killed by oil pollution in lagoons in Bristol, Connecticut. Fish and Game officials believe oil leaked from the fuel tank of a private home nearby. (Wide World)

We have used our creeks, rivers, and lakes as cheap sewers to carry away waste. (U.S. Department of the Interior)

that "running water purifies itself." Perhaps we simply didn't care. In any case we have used our creeks, rivers and lakes—the same ones from which we must draw much of our drinking water—as handy, cheap sewers to carry away every imaginable kind of waste.

We have filled our streams with raw excrement* and garbage,* laden with disease. We have stained

raw excrement—untreated human waste.

garbage—animal, vegetable, and kitchen refuse; different from rubbish such as paper or other objects (as from a garage).

them with oil, coal dust, tar, dyes, and chemical "liquors" discharged by industries. We have burned them with powerful acids which destroy all aquatic life except a stringy, loathsome type of algae.* We have turned them gray and murky with silt and sludge,* smothering shellfish and other forms of bottom life. We have used them to dispose of residues containing long-lasting poisons, some so powerful that less than one part per billion in a stream can kill fish. And, as though to show our contempt for our natural scene, we have dumped billions of tons of trash and offal* in our once lovely waters: beer cans, worn-out tires, old mattresses, rusty oil drums, refuse from hospitals, broken glass, dead animals, junked automobiles.

It is a dismal fact that we now have seriously contaminated and despoiled almost every creek, river, and bay in the entire United States. An early colonist called the graceful Potomac "the sweetest and greatest river I have seen," but in recent years a sign on the river landing below the green slopes and white pillars of Mount Vernon has warned visitors: DO NOT COME INTO CONTACT WITH POLLUTED WATER.

FURTHER INQUIRY

1. Why is water a primary source of life and wealth?
2. Are the waters near your home also becoming irreversibly polluted?

---

algae—form of seaweed silt.

sludge—sand and mud.

offal—parts of an animal that cannot be eaten.

Without a pure water supply, a city
dies. Because city water is becoming
filthier, cities have had to look farther
away for a clean water supply in order
to meet its needs. Costly though this
may be, it is essential to city life.

12

Water: Filthier
and Farther

by MITCHELL GORDON

"**E**VERY time you take a glass of water from
a faucet in St. Louis," says Richard Am-
berg, publisher of that city's morning *Globe-Demo-
crat,* "you are drinking from every flush toilet from
here to Minnesota."

The rival afternoon paper, the *Post-Dispatch,*
commented not long ago on a Public Health Service report concerning pollution of the Mississippi
in this manner: "The world's cleanest people, using
only the purest oils and spices in exorcising* grime

---

exorcising—getting rid of as if by magic.

From *Sick Cities,* by Mitchell Gordon. (New York: The Macmillan Co., 1963), pp. 84-85. Copyright © 1963 by Mitchell
Gordon. Reprinted by permission of The Macmillan Co.

To keep the beautiful Ohio River from becoming an open sewer for oily wastes, eight adjoining states have banded together to exert pressure on industry. (U.S. Department of the Interior)

witches, are drinking the garbage dump trickles of whatever town lies up the line. We bathe with scented fats and drink a factory's slime."

St. Louis is not unique among the nation's cities. A good many municipalities these days are drinking water that contains the inadequately treated discharge of communities upriver from them. And a good many more, from the looks of things, will be doing so in the future as water use increases along the nation's streams.

The prospect is not a pretty one. It was painted in vivid strokes some years back by Congressman Brent Spence, Kentucky Democrat: "I was born in sight of the Ohio River and I lived most of my life in a home that overlooked the river. I have seen it turn from a beautiful river in which I swam as a boy to a polluted sewer." The open sewer got so bad

that eight states finally banded together in 1948 to form the Ohio River Valley Sanitation Commission to clean up the stream. By mid-1962, over 1,000 cities representing all but 13 percent of the area's population had poured over $1 million into sanitation facilities, and the job still was not complete. The multi-state body hired a helicopter to film the dumping of oily wastes into the river by factories along its banks for showing to the general public, in the hope of pressuring industry into cleaning up its liquid waste before discarding it.

The tide, apparently, is finally being turned against the forces of pollution on the Ohio, but it is rising on a good many other waterways. The father of our country is fortunate he's not crossing the Potomac today. A joint House and Senate committee on the Capital's urban problems recently found the river so foul as to have become entirely uninhabitable to a wide variety of marine life that once thrived there.

Tulsa no longer draws water from the Arkansas River; it is so fouled with briny discharge. Chicago, which has spent over $400 million on sewage-treatment facilities to remove some 90 percent of the solids from its sewage, still disturbs communities as far as fifty miles downstream with its discard. And in Utah, contamination of the Great Salt Lake has become a matter of increasing concern to recreation-minded municipalities on that vast inland sea.

Authorities estimate well over 500 million pounds of solid wastes are pouring into the nation's waterways daily. Municipal sewer systems were already dumping twice as much waste into streams in 1961 as the maximum that was considered allowable as recently as 1955. A fourth of all the waste cities are sending into streams is raw sewage.* Another third is sewage that has had only the most cursory treatment. According to Dr. Abel Wolman, former chairman of the National Water Resources Board and more recently a top official of the National Research Council in Washington, D.C., practically every major waterway in the United States is now polluted in one degree or another.

FURTHER INQUIRY

1. To what extent are the water conditions in St. Louis similar to those in your city?
2. Why are cities using more water than ever before?
3. Why does the effort to "clean up" a river such as the Ohio require the cooperation of many states?

---

raw sewage—untreated sewage.

Some problems become more difficult to solve as time goes on. One such problem is the pollution of our waters. If neglected long enough, the problem may never be solved. If such should be the case it would be a national disaster. In this selection the author describes why the usual methods of dealing with water pollution are no longer successful.

13

Cool, Refreshing —and Filthy

by LEWIS HERBER

P RIOR to the Second World War, the United States had been undergoing a relatively slow, somewhat orderly transition from a rural to an urbanized society. As M. D. Hollis, Assistant Surgeon General, observes: "Cities were still separate entities. . . . Industries were in or near cities. Pol-

From the book, *Crisis in Our Cities* by Lewis Herber. Copyright © 1965 by Prentice-Hall, Inc. Published by Prentice-Hall, Inc., Englewood Cliffs, New Jersey. Reprinted with permission.

Sixty million gallons daily is the capacity of this sludge sewage treatment plant that serves a sixty-five square mile area. (Nassau County Department of Public Works)

lution . . . was natural organic materials* with concentrations of biological contaminants* (such as bacteria). Improvements in water treatment and extension of waste treatment kept the scales reasonably in balance. Excessive pollution, where it occurred, was still largely localized and over short stretches of streams."

A modern water-treatment plant is well equipped to cope with these conventional forms of waste. For the most part, its cleansing techniques are mechanical; they accelerate the natural purifying process that occurs in rivers. Before municipal sewage is discharged into a waterway, it passes through a simple

---

organic materials—made up of living things.

contaminants—substances which pollute.

An engineer operates the activated granular carbon columns through which effluent passes to remove dissolved organic materials. Then the effluent passes through the stack at left to remove dissolved inorganic ions. (U.S. Department of the Interior)

screen that catches large objects, while the liquid flows slowly through a series of tanks where sand, gravel, and organic solids (called "sludge") are permitted to settle to the bottom. In the final stages of treatment, the water is sprayed on a bed of rocks to remove any impurities produced by the action of bacteria and chlorinated. Much the same procedure is followed when the water is withdrawn from a river or lake for public use. In the past, these simple techniques, aided by the purifying processes in the waterway itself, sufficed to provide American communities with clean, safe, dependable drinking water.

But with the end of the war, the pace of urban and industrial development became a breathless dash. Cities began to expand at a breakneck pace, snaking along river banks for hundreds of miles and engulfing scores of towns and villages. The banks became heavily congested with homes and factories. A rash of entirely new industries appeared, producing an unprecedented variety of man-made chemicals.* . . . Today, hundreds of totally new chemicals are introduced every year into the American economy, and eventually, into the American water supply. Most of these synthetic chemicals are biologically unique; the human body has never had any experience in dealing with them physiologically. To complicate this problem, many of them are impossible to break down by conventional methods of water treatment.

Americans began to sense that they had entirely new pollution problems on their hands when the drinking water of some communities developed an

---

man-made chemicals—such as detergents and chemicals to help exterminate insects.

In a blanket of suds, these three brothers take a detergent swim in a stream near their home. When this same water comes from faucets in their home, it is most distasteful. (Don Rutledge, Black Star)

uncanny resemblance to beer. As early as 1947, a
detergent manufacturer appeared in a small Pennsylvania town, graciously offering free samples of
his product to all the local housewives. Two days
later, on a Monday, many housewives used the detergent in their weekly washes. Within hours, bil-
lows of detergent foamed up in the local sewage
treatment plant and were scattered around like snow.
Soon communities throughout the country began to complain that foam appeared from the kitchen
tap, the shower nozzle, and in the drinking glass.
The great detergent blizzard of the 1950's was finally underway.

Detergents are synthetic, highly stable cleansing
agents. In contrast to ordinary soap—a preparation
of vegetable and animal fats—they firmly resist de-
composition by bacteria and often pass through extremely fine filters. Although the synthetic cleansing
agents occasionally appear in the drinking water of
large communities, they have become the bane of
suburban homes. . . . By 1959, a large propor-
tion of such housing developments were afflicted by
detergents in drinking water. In Long Island, New
York, for example, the Suffolk County Department
of Health reported that more than a third of the 600
wells sampled by the agency contained detergents.
The Minnesota State Department of Health estimated that half of the 54,000 private wells
surveyed in the Minneapolis-St. Paul area are contaminated by the cleansing agents. As of this writing,
close to 1,000 bodies of well water in 13 states have
been examined for the presence of detergents. Nearly 40 percent contain synthetic cleansing agents in
varying levels of concentration.

A glass of water, heavily polluted by detergents,
is an insult not only to the palate and nostrils; as

drinking water, it is also an insult to the eyes. Agitate the water—and the cleansing agent forms a foam. But a large number of new pollutants are totally invisible; in low concentrations they are often tasteless and odorless. They appear in apparently clean water without furnishing the least evidence of their presence. No one, for instance, can possibly be aware of minute quantities of DDT in water. Even lethal* quantities of radioactive* material can enter the water supply and be consumed by the public without being immediately recognized. Indeed, millions of Americans, today, quench their thirst with cool, refreshing tap water in blissful ignorance that it contains an appalling, everchanging variety of industrial and agricultural chemicals.

FURTHER INQUIRY

1. Why is the problem of water pollution more difficult to solve than it once was?
2. Should housewives stop using detergents to wash clothes because detergents cannot be broken down as easily as soap?
3. What recommendations might you make to improve the drinking water of your community?

---

lethal—able to kill.

radioactive—rays emitted by atomic particles.

A huge, potential reservoir of pure water is ocean water. However, the fact that it is salty makes it unfit to drink. But what if the salt can be removed? Would we then have solved the nation's water problems? In this article the author reports on the largest desalination plant in the world. Desalination involves taking salt out of water and making it fit to drink. Why would this be a most important advance?

14

Water, Water Everywhere—and Now to Drink

by NEWSWEEK MAGAZINE

ON a bunting-draped* platform overlooking the briny Atlantic, a beaming Hubert H. Humphrey pushed a button and a plume of water shot from a nozzle into the air, catching the sunlight of late afternoon. "How do you like that?" cried the

bunting-draped—flag-draped.

From *Newsweek,* July 31, 1967. Copyright ©, Newsweek, Inc., July, 1967. Reprinted with permission.

Vice-President as a gay Key West crowd cheered. "That's fresh water. You can make lemonade out of it." Somebody handed him a green-tinted glass and he drank. "That's nice," he said. "Really nice. You just don't realize what a wonderful thing this is."

The plume of water, and the water in the glass, symbolized the formal opening last week of the nation's largest desalination plant, and the largest single-unit installation in the world. Built by the Westinghouse Electric Corp. at a cost of $3.3 million, its oil-fueled boilers and elaborate evaporation system already were producing 2,620,000 gallons of fresh water a day. And Key West, Florida, had become the first American city to be supplied with drinking water drawn from the sea.

No doubt the new plant would be dwarfed in the near future by nuclear powered installation—as Humphrey himself reminded the crowd, "There are much bigger things to come"—but the fact remained that Key West represented the longest practical step yet taken in the U.S. toward the utilization of ocean water to meet the needs of a large community. As one government official put it, "Key West has become a pathfinder of the world."

Growing Need: Actually, the world has already beaten a number of paths toward workable desalination. Every day, in at least twenty countries, salty or brackish* water is being turned into 100 million gallons of fresh water at some 200 plants, many of them U.S. built. In the U.S. alone, 359 desalting units of varying sizes are each producing an average of 25,000 gallons a day, some in coastal areas and drawing on the sea for small-scale community

---

brackish—polluted.

needs. Others in Arizona, inland Texas and Pennsylvania purify brackish or polluted water largely for industrial needs. But the product of the present plants is only a trickle of what will be needed to solve a problem that will have grown crucial within the next ten years.

It is not only that population grows while the water supply remains relatively constant. There is also the fact that in countries like the U.S., the amount of water used per capita has grown enormously since the turn of the century, partly because more people have bathrooms, but mostly as a result of industrial consumption. It takes 110,000 gallons of water to make a ton of steel, for example, and a jetliner needs 1,000 gallons to take off. In 1900, Americans used some 40 billion gallons of fresh water a day. By 1940, when the population had grown by only 74 percent, the usage of water had more than tripled. Today, the rate of consumption has soared to about 350 billion gallons a day—which is getting uneasily close to the country's potential water supply of 515 billion gallons.

FURTHER INQUIRY

1. What was unusual about the water Hubert Humphrey drank?
2. Why has desalination become more important than ever before?

The author of this speech is the former Surgeon General of the United States and, as such, is responsible for the nation's health. Here he argues that solving the problems of environmental health (air and water pollution) is urgent.

15

Environmental Health—the Time Is Now

by LUTHER L. TERRY, M.D.

THE urgency of our task is heightened by the fact that the problems are multiplying so rapidly. Twenty-one years ago, no one in Los Angeles had ever complained of smog; control measures were not instituted there until 1947. A dozen years ago, San Francisco was paying little attention to air pollution; today the San Francisco area has an ac-

Reproduced in Lewis Herber, *Crisis in Our Cities* (Englewood Cliffs, N.J.: Prentice-Hall, Inc., 1965), pp. 197-199. Copyright © 1965 by Prentice-Hall, Inc. Reprinted by permission.

tive control agency. In 1953, New York City had its first detected smog "episode," to which some 200 deaths are attributed. Washington, D. C., probably the least industrialized U. S. city of its size, had its first recorded instance of Los Angeles-type smog in June, 1960; there have been several more. One is reminded of the two little boys who were comparing their hands. "Mine's dirtier than yours," the first one said proudly. "Well," said the second, "you're a year older."

The population of the United States is increasing at an unprecedented rate. We now number more than 190 million, and our population is expected to increase to about 235 million by 1975. Urban areas are absorbing the increase. We expect that, by 1970, three out of four people will be living on only 10 percent of the land area of the United States. Thus, an increasing portion of the waste products discharged to the atmosphere will be released into relatively small segments of the air mass.

There is now nearly six times as much pollution in our rivers, streams and lakes as 60 years ago, and the amount is still increasing. An expanding population increases the demand for fresh water supply and, at the same time, increases the volume of waste. The crowding of people into urban centers intensifies the problems of waste disposal. Application of commercial fertilizers, and use of a vast array of new herbicides and insecticides,* contribute to pollution. Increased production of goods increases the amount of . . . wastes. New technologies produce new wastes that defy current ability to treat or control them and, in some instances, even to detect their

---

herbicides and insecticides—chemicals designed to kill unwanted plants and insects.

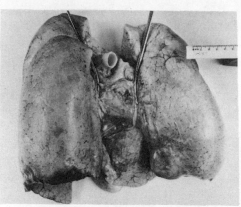

A healthy lung (top) and a diseased lung (bottom). Cigarettes and air pollution alike shrink our lungs, color them black, and shorten our lives. (R. J. Henning, St. Vincent's Hospital)

presence in water. Substances which are harmless in themselves react chemically with others to produce noxious odors and tastes.

Every year, more than 500 new chemicals and chemical compounds are introduced into industry. . . . Except with the most toxic materials, there is necessarily a time lag between the introduction of a new material or process and the recognition of deleterious effects. The lag is apt to be greater still where the effects are subtle, nonspecific deteriorations of general health and efficiency. The effect of occupational exposure is sometimes slow and undramatic, and may easily be mistaken for the "normal" process of deterioration which accompanies aging, for example.

. . . We have little exact knowledge of what takes place within the human body when it inhales, ingests, or comes into physical contact with toxic substances in small quantities over a long period of time.

All are inspired by the longing of the human spirit to free and ennoble itself so that man may live in harmony with the very forces of Creation with which he is seemingly at war. We are in danger, on the one hand, of creating an incredible disharmony in nature which will ultimately degrade and enslave us. Or we can create an environment which can enrich our lives, our society, and our individual well-being. It is for our generation to decide.

FURTHER INQUIRY

1. Why does the author say that problems of air and water pollution are more urgent than ever? How does greater concentration of people increase the problems of water supply and disposal?
2. Why are problems of air and water pollution multiplying rapidly?
3. Does new technology which has the capacity for producing new wastes also have the capacity to solve problems of air and water pollution? Justify your point of view.

Notes

Suggestions for
Additional Reading

Index

Notes

1. Quoted in Mitchell Gordon, *Sick Cities* (New York: The Macmillan Co., 1963), p. 84.
2. Ibid., p. 85.
3. Quoted in Edward Edelson and Fred Warshofsky, *Poisons in the Air* (New York: Pocket Books paperback edition, 1966), p. 53.
4. Public Health Service, *The Effects of Air Pollution* (Washington, D.C.: U.S. Dept. of Health, Education & Welfare, 1966).
5. Ibid.
6. Edward Edelson, *The Battle for Clean Air,* Public Affairs Pamphlet No. 403 (The Public Affairs Committee, Inc., 1967), p. 13.
7. Ibid., p. 15.
8. Ibid.
9. Lewis Herber, *Crisis in Our Cities* (Englewood Cliffs, N.J.: Prentice-Hall, Inc., 1965), p. 81.
10. Ibid., p. 86.
11. Rachel Carson, *Silent Spring* (Boston: Houghton Mifflin Company, 1962), p. 47.

12. L. Herber, op. cit., p. 92.

13. Ibid.

14. Edmund Faltermayer, "Can We Afford Cleaner Air?" *Fortune* Magazine, vol. 72, no. 5, Nov., 1965, p. 159.

15. Sylvia Porter, "Our Pollution Costs Sky-rocket," *The Trentonian.*

16. Ibid.

17. E. Faltermayer, Op. Cit.

18. *The New York Times,* Oct. 14, 1967, p. 29.

19. Prepared for Consolidated Edison Company of New York by Batten, Barton, Durstine & Osborn, Inc. (New York, 1967). Used with permission.

Suggestions for Additional Reading

1. Archer, Sellers. *Rain, Rivers, and Reservoirs: The Challenge of Running Water*. New York: Coward-McCann, 1963. A member of the Agriculture Department's Soil Conservation Services describes why we must conserve water and how it can be done.

2. Carhart, Arthur H. *Water—Or Your Life*. Rev. ed. New York: Lippincott, 1959. The twin problems of water shortage and pollution are still largely detached and unreal to many Americans whose "curiosity about water resources ends at the bathroom faucet." In this factual and alarming study the author explains the unbelievable mass of water uses and abuses which combine to create the problem of pollution.

3. Carr, Donald F. *Death of the Sweet Waters*. New York: W. W. Norton, 1966. Extremely readable, this is an account of the importance of water pollution control as a necessity for economic growth, public health, and recreation.

4. Graham, Frank, Jr. *Disaster by Default: Politics and Water Pollution*. New York: M. Evans, 1966. This is a reportorial but effective ac-

count of the water pollution problem in the United States. It is based on federal enforcement data and other government sources.

5. Herber, Lewis. *Crisis in Our Cities*. New Jersey: Prentice-Hall Inc., 1965. This contains a description of air and water pollution created by the growth of urbanization in the United States. The specific problems of some of America's greatest cities are here vividly described.

6. League of Women Voters Education Fund. *The Big Water Fight*. Brattleboro, Vt.: Stephen Greene, 1966. This is a highly readable account of the fight in various communities across the land for pure water. The book is an excellent record of the American people grappling with an urgent and complex situation in a democratic way.

7. U.S. Department of HEW. *Take Three Giant Steps*. Washington, D.C.: Division of Public Health Service, no. 1551, U.S. Government Printing Office, 1966. This booklet lists three steps an individual can take in solving the pollution problem.

8. U.S. Department of HEW. *The Struggle for Clean Water*. Washington, D.C.: Division of Public Health Service, no. 958, U.S. Government Printing Office, 1962. This booklet is an introduction to water pollution as a problem in conservation, health, and water resource management.

9. Warshofsky, Fred and Edward Edelson. *Poisons in the Air*. New York: Pocket Books Incorporated, 1966. This volume describes in clear

detail the poisons that are making the cities of America unlivable. It describes episodes when death lurked in the air and victims succumbed to air pollution.

10. Whalen, Richard J. *A City Destroying Itself*. New York: William Morrow and Company, 1965. This book describes New York City as a city that is destroying itself because of foul air and impure water. It is a call to action, to do something about an appalling situation that requires correction before it is too late.

Index

GENERAL EDITOR

Gerald Leinwand is Professor of Education and Chairman of the Department of Education at the Bernard M. Baruch College of the City University of New York. Dr. Leinwand received his B.A., M.S., and Ph.D. degrees from New York University and an M.A. from Columbia University. In addition to numerous magazine articles, he is the author of *The Pageant of World History, The American Constitution: A Tutor-Text,* and a college text *Teaching History and the Social Studies in Secondary Schools.*